gin
drinker's
toolkit

A Gelding Street Press book
An imprint of Rockpool Publishing
PO Box 252, Summer Hill, NSW 2130, Australia
geldingstreetpress.com

ISBN: 9781922662088

Published in 2024 by Rockpool Publishing
Copyright text © Mick Wüst 2024
Copyright design © Rockpool Publishing 2024

Design and typesetting by
Christine Armstrong, Rockpool Publishing
Illustrated by Ellie Grant
Publisher: Luke West, Rockpool Publishing
Edited by Heather Millar

All rights reserved. No part of this publication may be
reproduced, stored in a retrieval system, or transmitted
in any form or by any means, electronic, mechanical,
photocopying, recording or otherwise, without the
prior written permission of the publisher.

A catalogue record for this
book is available from the
National Library of Australia

A note about the measurements
Please note that the cup and spoon measures in
these recipes are based on Australian sizes.
1 teaspoon = 5 ml/$\frac{1}{6}$ fl oz
1 tablespoon = 20 ml/$\frac{2}{3}$ fl oz
1 cup = 250 ml/$8\frac{1}{3}$ fl oz

Printed and bound in China
10 9 8 7 6 5 4 3 2

gin drinker's toolkit

EQUIP YOURSELF TO NAVIGATE THE WORLD OF GIN

Mick Wüst

ILLUSTRATED BY ELLIE GRANT

This one goes out to my old gin club, Ginner Sanctum. The gins we tasted, the cocktails we invented, the conversations that slid seamlessly from theology to Firefly . . . it all led me here. Somehow.

Contents

introduction

Gin has the power to make you feel like James Bond or Audrey Hepburn.

This book is for anyone who likes gin, at least a little bit.

I don't mean anyone who's already a gin expert. You don't need an encyclopaedic knowledge of botanicals. Nor do you need a PhD in cocktail mixing, a handlebar moustache or a croquet set.

I mean anyone who enjoys a cheeky gin and tonic every now and then, or wants to master the art of the martini, or is curious about the hundreds of gins boasting exotic flavours from around the world. Anyone who's eager to experience new flavours and learn new things.

Gin's fairly simple at its core: a spirit infused with juniper berries along with other edible plants. Many of these botanicals are familiar ingredients – the lemons hanging on a tree in your granny's backyard, the rosemary growing in your local community garden, the cinnamon quill and star anise floating in a jug of mulled wine. Others may be less familiar, at least as ingredients in a drink – lavender belongs in soap, cucumber belongs in a salad, roses belong in a vase, and what on earth are cubeb berries?

But, still, gin is straightforward. You don't have to wait for a seasonal harvest like with wine, and it doesn't require years of ageing like whisky does. Even the word 'botanical' is just a fancy word for 'something from a plant'. And a G&T is one of the simplest drinks you can make – it's only two ingredients, for crying out loud!

Why complicate it with a whole book?

Because gin is beautifully simple . . . and stunningly complex. I remember my first gin. I was a teenager, the gin was Gordon's (snuck from my friend's mum), and it was mixed with Coke. I didn't appreciate spirits yet, and I knew nothing about gin. But I knew what Coke usually tasted like, and this was different. This was *better*.

I remember the first time gin made me truly smile. My wife and I were invited to the home of a couple from church, and our host casually served up a round of gin and tonics when we arrived. We were taken aback. We were in our early 20s, in that stage of life where money is scarce and people often bring their own drinks to gatherings. There was something about the way gin and friendship and generous hospitality all came together that imprinted on me. I remember sipping my G&T and thinking, 'If this is what adulthood is like . . . I think I like it.'

Then there's the first time gin made me laugh. My best friend ordered his first martini and asked for it dirty without knowing what that meant. He almost spat it out . . . poor guy didn't expect the taste of olive brine!

I remember my first gin cocktail, when some friends took me to a fancy gin bar.

The bartender asked me what I wanted, and I shrugged and said scotch was usually my spirit of choice. He thought for a moment, then invented a cocktail using a bourbon barrel-aged gin and a top-shelf sweet vermouth. It was definitely gin, but it was layered, and rich, and oily, and surprising. It took away any notion I had that gin is just one flavour.

When I hear someone say, 'All gin tastes the same,' I won't argue straight away. I'll concede that there is a certain gin-i-ness that juniper brings to London dry gin, and that once upon a time, most gins occupied a specific place on the flavour spectrum.

But then I'll start my monologue: about the variety of gin styles and botanicals, and the versatility of gin in cocktails, and the unique creative fingerprint of each distiller . . .

. . . at which point I realise the person has walked away, and I'm left standing alone.

Because let's be real here. Drinking gin is fun. Having someone ginsplain you is not fun. So if you're looking for someone to lecture you on London dry, pontificate about Plymouth, or natter on about navy strength gin, you're in the wrong place.

I'm not here to lecture. This isn't university.

This is junipersity.

(Did it work? Did you pronounce it juni-PER-sity in your head?)

At junipersity, we don't do lectures and textbooks and homework – at least, not in the traditional way. Our lectures are the chats we have with the bartender at our favourite bar, the discussions we have about flavour notes in our G&T, the questions we ask our local distiller. Our textbooks are the lists of botanicals on the labels of gin bottles, the flavour wheels we peek at while we're tasting our gin, the cocktail recipes we read and then promptly change to suit our tastes. And our homework? That's the best part. Trying different garnishes, organising a do-it-yourself gin tasting with friends, and hunting down new gins – oh, so many gins to taste!

Anyone can drink and enjoy gin without knowing all this special information (or should I say ginformation?). But I'm convinced that you appreciate gin even more if you're keen to learn about it. To go on an adventure with gin, seeking out more flavours and facts – just like the Dutch merchants who went sailing hundreds of years ago in search of more spices.

Winemakers talk about the terroir – that is, the sense of place – that grapes can bring to a wine. But while not everywhere can grow grapes, everywhere can grow *something*, and so gin can tell the story of *any* place with the taste of local and native botanicals.

Gin can derive its flavour from hundreds and thousands of different plants alongside juniper – a kaleidoscope of flavours. But there's more to gin than just the taste.

It's aesthetically pleasing. The elegant twist of an orange peel. The delicate V-shape of a martini glass. The shining copper and shimmering steam of a gin still, looking like a cross between a saxophone and one of those old diving suits.

It's a lesson in subtlety. The way a sprinkle of water can help gin to open up like a flower. The way ice can take the edge off an intense cocktail. The way botanicals reveal themselves in different ways, some tapdancing across your tongue at the start of the sip while others prefer a slow waltz towards the end.

It inspires feelings. When you sip a G&T, you feel relaxed and free. When you sip a martini, you feel stylish and sophisticated and powerful. When you sip a negroni, you feel the need to speak loudly and passionately and use lots of hand gestures.

It connects with nature. Spend time in a veggie garden, and you can develop an appreciation for the seeds and roots and leaves that go into gin. Taste a gin with Australian lemon myrtle, or Welsh pine needles, or Newfoundland seaweed, and you're tasting a certain place on earth. Flowers balanced on melting chunks of ice, oils from the peel of a fruit, the grain or grapes or potatoes that make up the base of your gin . . . these are all natural parts of our world, brought together in your glass.

It's anchored in history. You can follow gin's journey from the Netherlands, to London, to the rest of the world. You can join Winston Churchill with an ice-cold Plymouth gin, Frank Sinatra with a Tanqueray martini, or Queen Elizabeth II with a Gordon's and Dubonnet. You can drink cocktails invented by British naval officers, and tonic water invented when Peruvian cinchona bark was shipped to India, and gin made with spices that distillers slowly added to their repertoire over decades and centuries.

Of course, if I'd started with, 'Gin is more than a drink: it's beauty, and subtlety, and emotion, and nature, and history . . .' you would have slammed the book shut. But hopefully now you'll pour yourself a drink, experience it for yourself, and nod along as you read through these pages.

Or at the very least, you'll appreciate the pretty pictures and bad puns.

I'm confident there's a gin drink for everyone. Maybe this book will help you find your go-to way to drink gin – a drink that fits like a tailored tuxedo or a little black dress.

Or maybe you'll never stop exploring.

ASTOUNDING ADVENTURES OF
CAPTAIN GIN
THIS
THE MYS
CAPTAIN GI
STOR

section one

You can't spell 'origin story' without 'gin'.

When was gin first made? Where does gin come from, and where is it now? Who's making it, and who's drinking it? How is it made, and how did it get to where it is today? And why?

Well, we know why – it's bloody delicious.

History according to gin

Juniper grows rampant across Europe and has been valued for its medicinal properties for millennia. And people have been distilling alcohol for a long time, also often for medical purposes. It was only ever a matter of time before people brought the two together. Doctor's orders, of course.

Eventually, people started drinking juniper-infused booze for fun – like an early version of people enjoying the taste of cough syrup.

From there, things barrelled forward. I'm not game to suggest who first invented gin – Italy, Belgium and the Netherlands all fight for the title, and I don't want to be in the middle of it. But medical monks, a rhyming encyclopaedia and a merchant's cookbook all played a role in getting our favourite juniper spirit to where it is today.

In fact, gin has gone through quite the gauntlet over the years. It's been blamed for bringing London to its knees, it's been bought with gold dust, and it's been snubbed by Sean Connery. The English word 'gin' has been mocked by a philosopher, and it's been given the nicknames Dutch Courage and Mother's Ruin.

Let's travel back in time and catch a few glimpses of gin's history. Buckle in, save all questions until the end, and no drinking while the time machine is in motion, please.

Timeline

- **Circa 1550 BC** – In Egypt, the Ebers Papyrus lists juniper as a treatment for jaundice. It's one of the oldest existing records of medical practices from any culture.

- **77 AD** – Juniper meets booze – Roman naturalist and philosopher Pliny the Elder recommends juniper berries in wine as a diuretic and to remedy flatulence. (*insert toilet humour here*)

- **1055** – Benedictine monks in Salerno, Italy, use new technology from the Middle East to distil wine and use it to preserve juniper berries. This advancement in medicine is an exciting step towards gin.

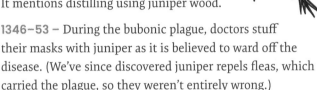

- **1266** – The first Dutch writing on distilling is in *Der Naturen Bloeme*, when Dutch poet Jacob van Maerlant translates a Flemish monk's natural history book . . . and makes it rhyme. It mentions distilling using juniper wood.

- **1346–53** – During the bubonic plague, doctors stuff their masks with juniper as it is believed to ward off the disease. (We've since discovered juniper repels fleas, which carried the plague, so they weren't entirely wrong.)

- **1351** – The first evidence of juniper-infused alcohol for recreational use, as opposed to medicinal. 'It makes people forget about sadness,' wrote Johannes de Aeltre, 'and makes their hearts happy and brave.'

- **1445** – A merchant in the Netherlands has a recipe for a spice-infused spirit including juniper in a handwritten household book. It's the earliest surviving recipe.

- **1522** – A doctor in Belgium, Phillipus Hermanni, publishes a recipe for wine infused with juniper berries and distilled to approximately 50% ABV – a kind of prototype recipe for genever.

- **1575** – The Bols distillery opens in Amsterdam, first producing liqueurs before launching genever in 1664. Today, Bols produces genevers, liqueurs, vodka and gin. It's the oldest distilling brand still operating in the world.

1568–1648 – The Eighty Years' War restricts grape supply in the Low Countries (which was already tough thanks to the Little Ice Age), so the base spirit of juniper drinks shifts from grape (wine) to grain.

1585 – Six thousand English soldiers go to aid the Dutch in the Eighty Years' War. They notice Dutch soldiers sipping from small bottles to give them fire in the belly as they fight. It's genever, or as the English call it: 'Dutch courage'.

1600 – English writer Sir Hugh Plat publishes *Delightes for Ladies*, which includes a recipe for a juniper-based spirit – evidence that juniper drinks are getting popular in London. By the end of this century, genever in England will evolve into gin.

1601 – Grain-based distilling is banned in the south of the Dutch Republic, driving Dutch distillers to leave and disperse their distilling techniques and recipes further afield. The ban won't be lifted until 1713.

1602 – The Dutch East India Company is launched, making Amsterdam a hub of world trade. Genever is sent around the world, and in return, more spices are imported than ever before, to the delight of distillers in the Netherlands – more botanicals to play with!

1638 – The Worshipful Company of Distillers is founded in London. To protect their secrets, they publish their manual *The Distiller of London* in code. Which is legen- wait for it . . .

1689 – King William III – a Dutch protestant – bans imported booze from Catholic France. The next year he abolishes taxes on grain-based distilling in England. The result? Gin production in England takes off like wildfire.

1714 – In *The Fable of the Bees*, Bernard Mandeville mocks the English shortening of the Dutch word *jeneverbes* (juniper) to a monosyllable. This is the first written use of the word 'gin'.

1720s–1750s – King William III's Distilling Act of 1690 worked too well. Within a generation, London is in the grip of the Gin Craze, and it's bad. Gin is made or sold in a quarter of all the houses in London, and it's dirt cheap. It gets the nickname 'Mother's Ruin', thanks to some awful things done by women who are addicted to gin, but men and even children are also guzzling the stuff.

1729 – English Parliament passes an Act to increase taxes on gin. It does nothing to slow down drinking. They pass another Gin Act in 1736. This doesn't help, either. The Acts stir up the masses to the point of rioting, forcing a reduction of gin taxes in another Act in 1743.

- **1736** – Captain Dudley Bradstreet sells gin illicitly with a sneaky trick: he hides in a house behind a sign in the shape of a cat, and when people put a coin in the cat's mouth, Dudley pours their gin through a pipe under the cat's paw.

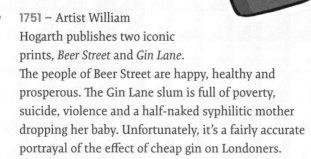

- **1751** – Artist William Hogarth publishes two iconic prints, *Beer Street* and *Gin Lane*. The people of Beer Street are happy, healthy and prosperous. The Gin Lane slum is full of poverty, suicide, violence and a half-naked syphilitic mother dropping her baby. Unfortunately, it's a fairly accurate portrayal of the effect of cheap gin on Londoners.

- **1751–60** – Yet another Gin Act is passed in 1751. In an attempt to reduce low-quality back-alley gin production, this Act says gin producers must have a certain size still, and must trade from more expensive venues. Together with the rising cost of grain, this Act finally slows the overconsumption of gin. The Gin Craze is over by the end of the decade.

- 1793 – The Black Friars Distillery is established in Plymouth, a naval dock town. While gin is losing popularity in London, it takes off with British Navy officers, who bring their dashing respectability to the drink.

- 1824 – The Surgeon-General of the Venezuelan army invents Angostura bitters as a cure for seasickness. To make it palatable, British sailors put it in their gin, and call the concoction 'pink gin'. Today, Angostura bitters is the most widely distributed bar ingredient in the world – and it still has that funny oversized label.

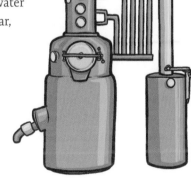

- 1825 – Over in India, British officers use a similar trick to make their malaria medicine easier to take. Their daily dose of bitter quinine-laced tonic water is improved with sugar, lime and gin.

- 1826 – Robert Stein develops the column still, but it's 1831 when Aeneas Coffey patents his updated (and more famous) design. The column still makes it easier and quicker and cheaper to produce clean neutral spirits. With no need to hide impurities, this leads to a drier style of gin (without sugar added), which evolves into London dry.

- **1850** – British Parliament eliminates duties on exported gin, enabling London distillers to distribute the new dry style worldwide.

- **1853** – Gin goes down under, as two ships carrying Gordon's gin arrive in port in Melbourne. The thirsty Aussies pay for the shipment in gold dust.

- **1858** – Englishman Erasmus Bond makes the first commercial tonic water. In 1870, Schweppes follows with their 'Indian Tonic Water'.

- **1862** – The first-ever cocktail book, *The Bar-Tenders Guide: How To Mix Drinks*, is published in the US by bartender Jerry Thomas. Over the next

century, American bartenders will invent a number of classic gin cocktails.

- 1870 – Fleischmann's distillery is established in Ohio. It's the first American distillery to produce a London dry gin.

- 1919 – In Florence, Italy, Count Negroni asks a bartender to make an Americano cocktail stronger by swapping the soda water for gin, thus inventing the negroni.

- 1920–33 – Prohibition kills small distilling in the USA, boosts sales for illegally imported British gin, and sends American bartenders scattering to places like Paris and London and taking their cocktail recipes with them.

- 1921 – In Kentucky, Maggie 'Queen of the Mountain Bootleggers' Bailey starts selling moonshine to support her family at just 17 years of age. Over the decades, she'll get to know the Fourth Amendment back-to-front to avoid searches and seizures, will become well-loved as a supporter of needy people in her community, and in her home county where it's illegal to sell alcohol she'll keep bootlegging until the age of 95.

- 1924 – Gordon's releases a range of pre-mixed cocktails in bottles shaped like cocktail shakers. The range is eventually discontinued, but the idea of a cocktail-shaker bottle returns . . . over at Tanqueray in 1948.

1939 – Canadian company Seagram jumps the border and begins making gin in Indiana (or Gindiana?). Seagram's will become one of the largest gin brands in the US and, despite its origins, an American icon.

1962 – James Bond drinks a vodka martini on the big screen (in *Dr No*), evidence that gin has fallen out of vogue. The art of bartending is in decline with the prevalence of soda guns, ice machines and pre-mixed drinks. The golden age of gin is over.

1986 – At a time when gin is seen as an old ladies' drink, Bombay Sapphire arrives on the scene in a cool blue bottle. It's less juniper-heavy and more citrussy, which helps it attract new gin drinkers. Gin is coming back with a facelift.

1993 – Plymouth Gin revives the kind of strong gin they used to make for the British Navy – which officers would test by mixing it with gunpowder to ensure it would still ignite – and coin the term 'navy strength'.

1995 – Tanqueray moves its production to Scotland. In 1998, Gordon's will follow. Beefeater finds itself to be the only historical gin still produced in London.

1996 – Having kicked off the craft spirits movement in the US by starting Anchor Distilling in 1993, Fritz Maytag launches the first craft gin since Prohibition: Junípero.

1999 – Hendrick's Gin is launched. It breaks the rules of London dry with its cucumber and rose petals added after distillation, but it wins the hearts of many.

2005 – Sick of preservatives and artificial sweeteners, a couple of savvy businessmen make Fever-Tree Indian Tonic Water – a natural and premium tonic water designed to do justice to quality gin.

2006 – Aviation Gin is launched. The way it downplays juniper and elevates other botanicals keeps it out of the London dry category. One of Aviation's founders, Ryan Magarian, writes an essay in 2009 to define this new category that includes gins like Hendrick's and Tanqueray No. 10. He calls it 'new western dry'.

2007 – Hayman's Distillers releases the first Old Tom gin available in the UK for over 40 years. This sweeter and older-style gin finds a market, since bartenders are looking back to classic cocktail books and the ingredients mentioned therein.

2008 – By coincidence, two distillers simultaneously release gins aged in wooden barrels – in France, Citadelle Réserve, and in the USA, Ransom Old Tom. They each do so in an attempt to create authentic historical flavours. What's old is new.

2009 – Sipsmith overturns a 250-year law (Gin Act of 1751) that prevents the opening of small distilleries, and is granted a distilling licence. It's the first distillery to open in London since 1820, and kicks off the craft gin movement in the UK.

2010 – Jonathan Adnams (of Adnams Brewery) challenges another long-standing UK law stating that brewers can't also distill on the same premises. He succeeds, and other craft brewers follow in his footsteps to produce craft spirits. Hops soon make their way into gins.

2016 – Gin marries wine when Australian distillery Four Pillars macerates shiraz (syrah) grapes in their gin to produce Bloody Shiraz – a world first.

2017 – In Japan, known for innovation in technology and precision in processes, Suntory releases Roku Gin. In India, associated with gin and the global spice trade for centuries, Nao Spirits releases India's first craft gin. Gin is taking over the globe.

2020 – . . . dary! Legendary! Anistatia Miller and Jared Brown, a quirky couple obsessed with booze history and mysteries, decipher the code from the 1638 book *The Distiller of London*, revealing early evidence of the spirit that would become known as gin.

2023 – The rise in cost of living around the world sees the gin category decrease as large distillers suffer losses and a number of craft distillers close. Many commentators declare the Ginaissance to be over. But as history has shown: gin never dies.

2024 – Drinks writer Mick Wüst is glad to see the back of the word 'Ginaissance'.

Gin today

For the most part, gin is a clear liquid. Pour it into a glass and it all looks the same. But looks can be deceiving – the variety in the world of gin is phenomenal.

Gin is an interesting mix of old and new, big and small, traditional and experimental; of holding tight to tradition and letting go of inhibition. There are gin brands that have been around for over 250 years, and new boutique brands launching all the time. There are gins that use botanicals from around the world, and gins made from wild plants foraged down the road from the distillery. There are gins that capture historically authentic styles and flavours, and novelty gins that barely fit the definition of gin.

It's an interesting mix. But it's all gin.

If you could go back to the early 1990s and tell people that gin will be even bigger than MC Hammer's pants, I wonder who'd believe you. Back then, the idea of World Gin Day, World Martini Day and Negroni Week would have been laughable. The gin section of a bottle shop was just a shelf – and the bottles were dusty. Nowadays, there's a whole wall of gins from across the globe. Those few iconic gins that existed before the age of CD-ROM are still around, but now the gin category isn't restricted to them. It's a flood that has burst its banks.

Gin boom

Call it the Gin Boom, call it the Ginaissance (if you must), call it whatever you want . . . but the 2000s and 2010s saw gin take off like no-one could have predicted.

How did we get from a handful of mostly British gin brands to thousands of distilleries worldwide? Just like any good twist of history, it involved a number of factors all coming together.

Tastes changed

When gin became unpopular in the 1950s and '60s (who wants to drink the same thing their parents are drinking?) vodka became the spirit *a jour*. Gin kept sinking in the '70s and '80s (who wants to drink the same thing their grandparents are drinking?) and flavoured vodka rose up and caught the attention of the cool kids.

But these flavoured vodkas actually paved the way for gins that didn't taste like traditional gins, like the citrussy Bombay Sapphire, the cucumber and rose infused Hendrick's, and the zesty and floral Tanqueray No. 10.

And the vodka drinkers who didn't like the juniper-heavy taste of traditional gins? Well, they found these new gins suited them just fine. They became a new generation of gin drinkers, which inspired a new generation of gin makers.

The cynical among us may wonder if those pioneering new gins were less driven by passionate gin makers, and more by large corporations and clever marketing teams chasing the flavoured vodka drinkers.

But even if these gins began as a way to reach the less adventurous, the irony is that they opened up the world of gin to more adventurous gins that explore a broader part of the flavour spectrum.

Laws changed

Rules that make things easier for those in power seem to come around quite easily, and have a habit of sticking around. But changing these rules so creative entrepreneurs can try new things? This doesn't happen unless individuals fight to bring about change.

In America, regulations around distilling popped up at the end of Prohibition in the 1930s – and stuck around for decades. These rules worked just fine for the huge corporate distillers, but not so much for up-and-comers who wanted to make small batch spirits. In the '70s and '80s (and onwards), some determined distillers stood up and fought to change these regulations, and their achievements made the craft spirits movement possible for everyone who came after them. In 1996, Anchor Distilling's

Junípero was the first craft gin in America since Prohibition and was referred to as 'the gin that launched a thousand craft gins'.

In the UK, the laws that tied the hands of distillers were even older – they'd been in place since the infamous Gin Craze of the mid-1700s. Again, the large distilleries had managed to get by without issue, but it took serious lobbying in the 2000s for people to get permission to start small distilleries. In the end, a potato farmer (William Chase, who made Tyrells potato crisps and Chase Distillery potato vodka) and the Sipsmith Gin crew are to thank for their persistence – they were trailblazers who smoothed the way for all who would follow in their footsteps.

Of course, this is just the story of two countries – but the US and UK gin industries were both hugely influential in the explosion of new distillers around the world.

Beer and whisky and cocktails changed

At a time when the beer industry was ruled by a few massive breweries whose beer tasted the same, the craft beer movement showed drinkers that beer could be different, and beautiful, and made by a small team of passionate makers rather than a giant factory. It didn't take long for a few imaginative gin lovers to look at this and ask, 'Why couldn't we make gin differently to the big guys, too? Why couldn't we have a craft gin movement?'

At a time when new distilleries started popping up with a focus on whisky, those whisky distillers faced an obstacle: 'Whisky takes years to mature. How can this business survive between when we first make the spirit and when we can sell it?' Their answer was to make other spirits on the side to provide cashflow – namely, vodka and gin. 'Less interesting,' thought the whisky lovers, 'but a necessary evil.' But as they waited for their whisky to be ready, many of these distillers fell in love with gin. They experimented with botanicals and strived to perfect their craft. Suddenly, there was a wave of great gin available, and drinkers found it – and they fell in love with it, too.

At a time when cocktails were evolving from the colourful and sweet and stupidly named drinks of the '80s and '90s (Screaming Multiple Orgasm On The Beach, anyone?) into an art form focused on quality spirits and classic combinations, bartenders wanted better ingredients. They were no longer satisfied with the mass-produced bottom-shelf spirits. They were making elegant drinks, so they wanted the boutique spirits that showed the heart and soul of the distiller. They wanted fresh flavours they could use to create high-end cocktails for their classy cocktail bars. They wanted historical spirits that matched the recipes in their 100-year-old cocktail books (and the olde-timey waistcoats they'd all started wearing). And when they looked to *The Bar-Tender's Guide* from 1862 and *The Savoy Cocktail Book* from 1930, what's one of the spirits they saw listed again and again? You guessed it – gin.

Big gin vs small gin

Distilleries come in all shapes and sizes. Each has its own set-up that looks different to their neighbour down the road. But for better or worse, many people divide them into two general size categories – big or small. And there's a lot of weight to these words.

Big gin

Mass-produced gin. Commercial gin. Large distillers. Whatever you call them, these are the whales of the gin ecosystem.

We're talking distilleries that put out millions of bottles of gin every year. We're talking large-scale machinery and global exportation. And we're talking distilleries owned by corporate groups with multiple brands in their portfolios: Gordon's, Tanqueray, and Seagram's are owned by Diageo; Beefeater and Plymouth are owned by Pernod-Ricard; Bombay Sapphire is owned by Bacardi; and Hendrick's is owned by William Grant & Sons.

With their massive production, marketing and distribution, big gin sells far more volume than thousands of smaller distilleries combined. They're also able to sell at a lower price – if you hear people referring to 'rail gin', 'house gin' or 'bottom-shelf gin',

they're referring to a lower cost product from one of the large distillers – the kind of gin that bars use in their mixed drinks. Cheap and cheerful.

People sometimes talk about large companies like they're completely soulless. Like maybe they boil children in vats when people aren't looking. But corporate ownership and factory production aren't necessarily bad, and don't always equal a lack of character when it comes to gin. Many distilleries retain a strong sense of history and place, even after they're acquired by The Big Guys.

Zoom in on multinational corporation Pernod-Ricard, for example, and you'll see their brands include a British gin made on the same site since 1793, an Italian gin made with Sicilian citrus and Piedmont water, a Canadian gin made with local corn spirit and hand-foraged botanicals, a German gin made with water and botanicals from the Black Forest, and a Japanese gin made from rice spirit with bamboo and yuzu in the mix. If a cynical drinker ever says to you, 'They probably all come out of the same factory,' invite them to look a little closer.

Size does matter

Bigger isn't just a matter of size. At a larger scale, all kinds of things change.

For example, at Bombay Sapphire, they need to stir thousands of litres of gin at a time to make sure they're getting an even, consistent flavour. But they can't use a mechanical paddle that might make a spark and cause an explosion, and no-one's volunteering to get in there with a wooden spoon. So how do they mix the gin? They release a three-metre-wide bubble of nitrogen into the bottom of the tank, which stirs up the liquid as it rises.

Small gin

Craft gin. Small batch gin. Independent distillery. Boutique distillery, artisan distillery, microdistillery, local distillery. These are all describing basically the same section of the gin market – the thousands of distilleries that aren't 'big gin'. In the gin ecosystem, these are everything from the tiny herrings to the sizeable tuna . . . with a few colourful starfish, flappy stingrays and weirdo octopuses thrown in there.

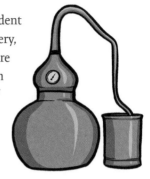

The United States led the craft gin boom from the mid-1990s, but it didn't take long for independent distillers to start popping up in England, Canada, continental Europe, South America and New Zealand. And I'll gladly boast that Australia punches above its weight in numbers of distillers and worldwide acclaim.

There's no clear agreement on what a 'craft gin' is, or how small is 'small batch', or if a distiller loses street cred for selling a share of their company. But there are a number of markers that work together to create a certain vibe.

With a craft gin, you'll probably be able to tell who's behind it. It's often one distiller, or a couple, or a small group of people. Their faces and names are easy to find on the company's website, where they'll also tell their story of how and why they got into gin in the first place. Usually, it's a story of passion before profit.

Depending on the distillery size, there's probably the same person sticking with a batch of gin from start to finish. This person is involved through the whole process, from choosing the botanicals, to distilling the gin, to diluting the distillate, to quality control. They're the one cleaning the gunk out of the still at the end, too. I was chatting with the owner of a local distillery recently, and while we spoke, he was choosing the coloured wax he was going to hand-dip each bottle into. This is worlds apart from a large factory with an assembly line approach, where each member of the production team is only involved in one section of the gin-making process.

Craft gin may vary from batch to batch. Whether that's positive or negative is each person's opinion, but every batch can have its own character as the distiller continues to tweak their recipes and botanicals.

With smaller batches, it's often easier for the distiller to experiment. There's less risk associated with 500 litres than with 5000 litres, so craft distillers can have fun with limited release gins and see how their customers respond.

These distillers are usually transparent about what's in their gin, and how they made it. Part of the joy of being an artisan is sharing your art with others, so craft distillers will list their botanicals, explain the gin-making process and invite people to come into the distillery.

Small distilleries are part of their local community. They collaborate with fruit farmers, hire local artists to design their labels, invite community groups to have a tour of the distillery, run stalls at the Sunday markets and sponsor local sports teams.

The big players have started to take on some of these traits – such as experimental flavours and transparency in botanicals – but on the whole, the more of these markers that you notice in a particular gin or distillery, the more likely you're looking at a craft gin.

At the liquid level, I don't think the divide between big gin and small gin is always significant. I've heard people speak as though small gin is good and big gin is bad . . . but it's not that simple. There are apathetic people in small distilleries making mediocre products, and there are passionate people in large distilleries who are constantly innovating and experimenting.

Having said that, I do love small distillers. I'm all for buying locally made products, supporting small businesses run by passionate people, and encouraging small distillers to grow and experiment. Do this, and gin will continue the charge forward!

Gin around the world

Gin is inextricably linked to English history and culture. Many of us have a picture in our heads of the royal family playing croquet, eating cucumber sandwiches and sipping G&Ts. (Please tell me that's not just me.)

But while the UK is still the epicentre of gin, being home to more distilleries than anywhere else and boasting the oldest gin brands in the world, gin isn't confined to the British Isles. It's now made in well over 100 countries around the world.

The Netherlands is home to genever, the malty juniper spirit that preceded gin . . . though Belgium may fight them for the title. Will you have your ice-cold genever with a beer chaser, or accompanied by a salt-dried green herring?

Italy may be known for wine, but it claims to have made the first gin-like drink, and definitely gets full credit for the negroni. Enjoy one as an aperitif as the sun sets.

In Spain, they've taken gin and tonic – or should I say, *gin tonica* – to a new level, inspiring gin lovers around the world with the image of a *copa de balon* glass full of ice and multiple garnishes. (The Spanish habit of drinking gin with cola hasn't gone global to the same degree.)

In Kenya, the native species African juniper (*Juniperus procera*) has made its way into gin alongside botanicals from across the continent like Moroccan coriander, Madagascan pink peppercorn and Kenyan green tea.

A mere 9000km south and a smidge east of London, South Africa has fallen in love with gin. Many feature botanicals of the Cape, like earthy rooibos and vibrant flowers from native fynbos plants.

America has come a long way since the bathtub gin of Prohibition. The craft gin movement in the US is characterised by bold, assertive flavours. Coriander-forward gins, cardamom-forward gins, lavender-forward gins . . . you name it, and there's a US gin focusing on it.

The Philippines holds the title for drinking more gin than any other country. Filipinos love standing around on the street on a warm evening for a *ginuman* (gin drinking session), with their hand wrapped around a cold *ginpo* – gin, pomelo juice and ice.

The national drink of Singapore is a Singapore sling, a pink, fruity and herbal cocktail that's over 100 years old. Sit at the famous Long Bar at Raffles, drink a Singapore sling (at tourist prices), and throw your peanut shells on the floor of the bar.

Australia has made a name for itself on the world gin stage – partly for its many award-winning gins, partly for a gin that's steeped with shiraz wine grapes . . . and partly for a gin containing green ants. Ew.

From Norway, where juniper branches feature in beer even while the berries flavour gin, to India, where the gin scene is steaming forward with an unsurprising mastery of spices. From Ireland, where you can drink shamrock-infused gin, to Switzerland, where the gin sparkles with glacial water and edelweiss (the flower, not the song from *The Sound of Music*). From the delicate flavours of Japan to the desert botanicals of Mexico. From a French distiller putting pickles in your gin to a Canadian distiller putting lobsters in your gin.

Gin has truly become a global drink. You know what they say: 'You can take the London dry out of London, but you can't take the gin out of . . .' Hang on, that's not right. 'You can't take the dry . . .' Wait, let me try again. 'A London, a dry and a gin walk into a bar . . .'

Okay, it turns out I don't know what they say.

Ingredients of gin

Some haters say gin is 'just vodka with berries and stuff in it'. They're not entirely wrong, just as you wouldn't be entirely wrong if you said pizza is 'just bread with tomato and stuff on it', or the *Mona Lisa* is 'just wood with some paint on it'.

When it comes to making gin, that 'vodka' the haters referred to is the base spirit or neutral spirit.

Juniper berries are the star ingredient – they belong in every single bottle of gin. But each gin is a tapestry, and many other botanicals help make up the intricate patterns of aroma and flavour. The list of options is basically every plant on the planet, though distillers tend to avoid the disgusting and the poisonous. Who knows why?

Base spirit

When we talk about gin, we're forever talking about juniper and botanicals. But on their own they'd make some kind of dukkah or potpourri, not gin. For them to become gin, they need liquid, and that liquid is the base spirit.

Base spirit is what gin makers re-distil with juniper and other botanicals. It's super high in alcohol, usually clocking in at over 95% ABV (in the EU, it's a legal requirement that the base spirit for gin is at least 96% ABV). The point of this spirit is to bring the booze, not the taste; it's almost pure ethanol and it's close to flavourless, with everything that brings flavour having been stripped out during the distillation process. That's why it's often called 'neutral spirit'. Not the most romantic of names, but it gets the job done.

What's ABV? What's proof?

ABV refers to the Alcohol by Volume. It measures the alcohol content of a liquid as a percentage. Simple.

In the USA, many spirits have a 'proof' measurement on the label, which is double the ABV. An 80 proof gin is 40% ABV, a 114 proof gin is 57% ABV, a 192 proof neutral spirit is . . . well, you take the point.

Internationally, ABV seems to cause the least confusion.

It's common for distillers to see the botanicals as the most important or creative part of making gin, so many don't give much consideration to the base spirit they use. After all, it's just neutral, right? As long as they can make gin with it, they're happy.

But if you take a moment to look at this transparent liquid, you'll see there's more than meets the eye . . .

It can be made of anything

For some spirits, the ingredients they're distilled from is what defines them. Whisky's made from malted grains, grappa is made from grapes, rum's made from sugarcane, and mezcal's made from agave.

But gin gets its identity from juniper, not from the origin of its spirit.

Base spirit made from barley? You can make gin with that.
Base spirit made from grapes? You can make gin with that.
Base spirit made from milk or whey? You can make gin with that.
Base spirit made from sugarcane, or rye, or potatoes, or apples, or . . . you get the idea.

It can be flavourless, or it can have character

If a ginsmith is all about the botanicals, they may want their base spirit to be as flavourless as possible – a blank canvas on which they can paint their botanical masterpiece.

But others may decide to use a more distinctive spirit. Not all 'neutral spirit' is entirely neutral; it may be 96% pure ethanol, but that remaining 4% can make a difference to the taste. A distiller might go with one spirit over another based on the slight character it brings. The differences are subtle but, hey – making gin is all about subtlety.

Some distillers don't not choose their neutral spirit based on how flavourless or otherwise it is, but simply use what's available. A bourbon distillery that already has corn aplenty? A distillery in the Caribbean where sugarcane is an abundant crop? A gin maker surrounded by cider makers? In cases like these, the ginsmith is just using what's around. A good gin maker will work with the nuances of their base spirit to give their gin panache, personality, a certain *je ne sais quoi*.

Most gin makers don't make their own base spirit

We like to think artisans make everything from scratch, but not all gin distillers make their own base spirit. In the same way that many sandwich shops buy in their bread, many gin makers buy neutral grain spirit from large industrial suppliers.

Part of the reason for this is a holdover from centuries of UK law that required base spirit to be distilled in a separate place to where it was turned into gin. Tax laws have shaped a lot of booze history!

But, also, making 96% ABV neutral spirit isn't practical for many gin makers, especially the smaller producers. It requires a lot more equipment (you need your own brewery!), more space, more money. It takes more labour, skill and time. It means more paperwork, approvals and taxes. And even after jumping through all those hoops, most small producers still couldn't make a neutral spirit as clean as the industrial producers can.

If you're tempted to give these makers a hard time, consider this: how many artists do you know who make their own canvases?

Maybe in the future we'll see more ginsmiths making their own base spirit. But for now, rest assured that the availability of cheap, high-quality neutral grain spirit means we have far more gin producers, which leads to more experimentation, more innovation and more variety in the world of gin. Raise your glass to that!

Juniper

If you want to understand wine better, it makes sense to learn something about grapes. If you want to understand whisky better, it makes sense to learn about barrels. And if you want to understand gin better, it makes sense to learn about juniper.

Juniper is the heart and soul of gin. You may not know anything else about this funny little berry, but without juniper, there is no gin.

What is juniper?

Juniper isn't just a word on an ingredients list; it's a plant.

There are over 50 species of juniper. The one you'll usually find in gin is *Juniperus communis,* or the common juniper, though some distilleries play around with different varieties. *¡Viva la experimentación!*

Common juniper has a massive spread across the northern hemisphere, like someone got a map of the world and a broad paintbrush and smeared juniper all the way across Europe, Asia and North America. It can thrive in lush conifer forests, on open snowy plains and in rocky crevices out in the hot sun. It's a real trooper.

This shrub has spiky needle-like leaves and blue-black berries. They look like blueberries from a distance, but up close you'll see they're knobbly. That's because they're not actually berries, but small cones with fleshy scales that fuse together. (We can still call them berries, though. They don't mind.) Inside each cone-or-berry, you'll find one to three seeds full of aromatic oils. This is the part distillers are really, really interested in.

Just as the flavour of wine grapes can change based on the soil and climate of where they're grown, so too can juniper, so each gin distiller chooses carefully where they get their berries from. Even today, a lot of juniper is harvested in the wild by people who collect them, dry them out, and sell them to a spice company. With the moisture dried up and the precious oils locked up safely inside the seeds, dried juniper berries can be stored for two or three years before their flavour drops.

What part does it play in gin?

You probably don't want to chomp down on a juniper berry – the strong pine taste and citrus-like bitterness make for an intense experience. But take that intensity and put it in gin with a bunch of other botanicals? You're in flavour country.

In the world of gin, there's a huge spectrum of nuance thanks to the near-endless range of botanicals available. But all gins still have a certain gin-i-ness. That's largely because of the juniper. It doesn't just have one flavour, though; it's helpful to talk about the *flavours* of juniper. In the same way that chocolate and coffee flavours blend together to make mocha, the aromatic compounds in juniper berries bring a combination of flavours that blend together to give that juniper-i-ness.

Even though juniper has many facets, it has a fairly distinct signature. The complex blend of flavours can lean more one way or another, but in general, it goes something like this . . .

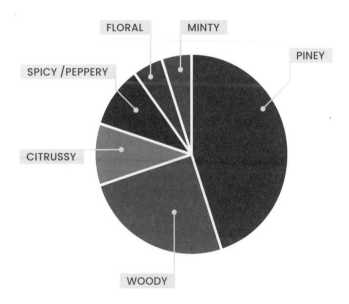

When you notice the different flavours in juniper, suddenly it makes so much sense how other botanicals can either highlight these flavours or contrast with them.

The science of flavour

Flavour scientists (yes, that is a thing) have isolated the molecules that give each botanical its aromas and flavours.

The leading flavour molecule in juniper is alpha-pinene, which has that pine, spruce, almost antiseptic taste. But there's also sabinene (woody, spicy), limonene (citrussy), farnesene (floral), borneol (woody), beta-myrcene (spicy, earthy, musky), cineole (minty), germacrene D (herbal) and a whole chorus of others.

When it comes to other botanicals, coriander seed picks up on the alpha-pinene, borneol and limonene; citrus peel has a strong limonene presence; and many herbs are loaded with germacrene D.

Gin makers have always known these botanicals go well with juniper; now scientists can explain why!

Other botanicals

When you hear the word 'botanicals', what do you think of? A botanist's leather-bound notebook, full of sketches of exotic plants she's spotted as she travels to distant lands aboard a wooden ship? Or the potion recipes of a witch or druid, written on a scroll in curly script, listing the marvellous and magical properties of each plant?

Botanicals aren't a mystery; the word 'botanical' just means something from a plant. Fruits and flowers, seeds and nuts, roots and leaves, herbs and spices.

Juniper berries are the backbone of gin's signature flavour, but there are other bones too. Each botanical plays a unique role in the flavour profile of a gin. Even when two botanicals seem similar, they're not interchangeable; each one contains its own combination of oils and acids that interact with other botanicals and with our senses. For example, coriander seed and citrus peel both bring a citrussy flavour, but the volatile oils of the peel hit your tastebuds up front while the coriander brings its citrus-like flavour towards the finish. Distillers often use them in unison to stretch out the citrus experience through the entire sip – an effect that neither ingredient could do on its own.

Gin makers often look to a pool of tried-and-tested ingredients because they work so well; a kind of 'if it ain't broke, don't fix it' approach. But any edible plant is fair game when it comes to making gin.

Very common

Coriander

If juniper is Batman, coriander is Robin. Upward of 80% of gins feature coriander, which makes this sidekick the most important contributor to gin's flavour profile after our hero.

Don't stress if you're someone who hates coriander leaf (aka cilantro) – when it comes to gin, we're talking about the seed of the plant. Entirely different flavour.

Coriander is best known for the citrussy notes it brings to the back end of a gin, but it's a complex mix of characteristics – spicy and herbal, floral and fruity. As with juniper, terroir matters with coriander – it varies based on where it's grown, so distillers should know where their coriander is from.

Angelica

With the excellent scientific name *Angelica archangelica* (and the less exciting alias 'wild celery'), this plant is used in so many gins that it can be hard to pick out from the flavours of juniper and coriander.

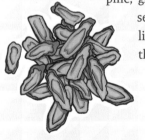

Angelica root is a walk through the forest – think pine, green herbs and damp wood – while its seeds can be used for their floral and hop-like notes. Occasionally a distiller will even throw the flowers in for good measure.

Along with orris root, angelica has traditionally been added to 'fix' other ingredients – that is, to help their aromas stick around for longer. There's no scientific evidence for this . . . but who are we to argue with distillers?

Lemon and orange

They say the key to winning a fistfight is to hit first and hit hard. If that's true, citrus would never lose.

The volatile oils from lemon or orange peel give a zip and zing up front, even if they also make their exit quickly. Lemon begins as a candy-like or sherbetty character before shifting to the taste of freshly grated zest. Bittersweet Seville oranges used to be the norm, but in recent years, the sweet Valencia orange has been having its time in the sun (figuratively – it's often used fresh, not dried).

Dried peel is the most common way to use citrus. Back in the day, distillers had more reliable access to dried peel than fresh citrus, since it was easier to ship over long distances and store all year round.

Orris root

Orris root is the bulb of the sweet iris plant, and it's a hard-won ingredient – it's harvested by hand after three or four years, then dried for up to five years to bring out the character of its oils.

While it's traditionally used in perfumes and gins for its supposed ability to fix aromas, this botanical is worth it for its complex aromatic notes alone. Imagine the sweet hay and dry earth smell of clean stables, then bring in the perfume of a big bunch of violets.

Its oils are slow to evaporate, so orris's character comes late and lasts long on the palate.

Cassia and cinnamon

Cassia and true cinnamon are two different species, though they're sometimes used interchangeably. Think of them as lookalike siblings – often mistaken for each other, but get to know them and you can appreciate their differences. They both have earthy, warm and sweet personalities, but cassia is a bold brute while true cinnamon is a more delicate soul.

Cardamom

Cardamom has long been a key ingredient of chai tea, but more recently these pods have gained popularity in the world of gin, with their part-peppery, part-floral and part-fruity character.

Green cardamom is used more commonly for its pungent eucalyptus and citrus punch, but black cardamom is sometimes used for its smokier finish.

Liquorice root

You might expect liquorice root to bring the taste of liquorice to a gin. You'd be wrong. If a distiller wants a liquorice-y flavour in their gin, they'll add fennel seed, star anise or aniseed.

So what do they use this for? Sweetness. Liquorice root is about 50 times sweeter than sugar – a little goes a long way.

Liquorice root can also impart its woody and earthy flavour and a soft, almost oily texture . . . but mostly it's the sweetness distillers are after.

Common

The signature tastes of **almonds** are marzipan and nuttiness, but these kernels are prized for the texture they add to gin – a soft, almost creamy mouthfeel.

The sweet spiciness of **nutmeg** is warming, earthy and dry. It's the snuggly warm blanket of spices, with a comforting aroma that reminds me of banana bread or spiced cookies baking in the oven. Apparently, it's also an aphrodisiac, so enjoy that lingering warmth.

Cubeb berries are in the same family as pepper, and they certainly bring pepperiness to a gin's aroma. But they're a shapeshifter – depending on what they're paired with, they can offer up lavender, lemon, pine or alpine mint.

With a fiery taste, **grains of paradise** are sometimes used as a less harsh alternative to pepper, but they also bring hints of lavender that tie in with juniper, a citrussy spice to boost coriander, and a menthol warmth that goes with cardamom. Their name was a mediaeval marketing trick – they're from West Africa, but spice traders claimed these seeds only grew in the Garden of Eden.

All kinds of citrus are used in gin. Pink grapefruit peel brings a zesty and bittersweet quality. Yuzu is wrinkly, lumpy and ugly, but this East Asian fruit's skin is full of beautiful oils. Finger lime is a native Australian fruit known for its aesthetics as much as for its limey taste – cut one open and watch the juicy globules ooze out like caviar. There's also bright mandarin, sweet and juicy tangelo, intense and spicy kaffir lime leaves, delicate orange blossom . . . no citrus is safe from gin distillers.

Peppercorns sound straightforward, but they're really not. Black peppercorns are the ones on everyone's dining table and bring their dusty heat and tart pungency to gin. But 'pink peppercorns' can refer to three species that all taste different . . . and none of them is related to black pepper.

Love it or hate it, it's hard to ignore **ginger**. Its intense warmth is comforting when used with baking spices, and its dryness is a welcome partner to zesty citrus notes.

Elderflowers give a fresh honey-like note, while **elderberries** bring a tart jammy flavour. In *Monty Python and the Holy Grail*, elderberries are a silly French insult: 'Your father smelt of elderberries!'

Lavender has been used in soaps and perfumes for millennia, and in recent times its soft floral scent has found its place in gin (especially American gins).

Aniseed, **star anise** and **fennel seed** – these three botanicals are from different plants, but they're all excellent at mimicking the dark, spicy flavour of liquorice.

Sloes are often called sloe berries because they look similar to blueberries (and juniper!), but they're actually stone fruit related to plums and cherries. When they're used to make sloe gin, they provide that luxurious reddish-purple colour and the sour-sweet flavour of pomegranate, cranberry or sour cherry, along with a little almond character.

Less common

Gin must contain juniper, but apart from that, it's a free-for-all. Distillers aren't limited to some list of allowed botanicals; they can make use of anything in the plant kingdom. Here's a random assortment.

If you think **cucumber** is only good for salad – or not even good then – I implore you to keep an open mind here. Cucumber brings a light melony freshness that lifts the spirits.

Hops aren't new to gin, but the craft beer boom has made these leafy green cones more understood and accessible to non-brewers. Hops can evoke flavours including grass, pine, stone fruit, bright citrus, soft florals, tangy passionfruit and dank cannabis.

Sweet, rich and fragrant, **saffron** is the most expensive spice in the world. Saffron threads are hand-picked from crocus flowers, and it takes over 100,000 flowers to yield a single kilogram of the spice. Forget gold – invest in saffron! (Please don't actually take financial advice from this book.)

Gins containing **butterfly pea flower** are a rich blueish-purple hue, and even change colour when you add tonic water. Magic!

For many of us, **rosemary** is reserved for roast dinners and Mediterranean dishes. But the sticky, piney and savoury character of rosemary can be a welcome addition to the late taste of a gin.

Chamomile flowers look like daisies and are best known for being dried and made into a tea that helps you sleep. In gin, they bring a soft floral note that sits among the other flavours like a sweet, fluffy teddy bear.

You don't get a prize for describing what **lemongrass** tastes like: it's lemony and grassy. It goes superbly with the dry heat of ginger, in Asian food and in gin.

The world of plants is vast; distillers aren't going to run out of ideas or flavours any time soon. They can look to other herbs like dill, mint, sage and thyme; other flowers like hibiscus, honeysuckle, jasmine and rose; other fruits like plums, strawberries, raspberries and lingonberries.

There are gins with unusual botanicals like asparagus, cactus, coconut and seaweed. There are also gins containing ingredients that technically aren't botanicals: ingredients like shiraz, cream, truffles, gold flakes, lobsters and green ants.

You know . . . totally normal things.

Making gin

When you hear that dodgy publicans made gin in bathtubs during Prohibition, you think: 'How complicated could it be?'

Then you hear about illegal distillers causing an explosion, or people going blind from drinking bad moonshine, and think, 'Hmmm. Maybe there's more to it than I realised.'

It's not easy to make gin. It's harder again to make it taste nice. That's why we love those distillers who do it for us. They're flavour experts, chemists, engineers and mad scientists. They sweat and toil with machinery and dried spices and high-tech gadgets so we can drink G&Ts on the patio in the sunshine.

A non-distiller's guide to making gin

I'm no distiller, and I'm no scientist. In high school science class, I was the kid drawing stick figure comics in my notebook. But making gin is more interesting than science class.

When I started working on this book, I hung out with a distiller for hours while he made a batch of gin: feeling the heat coming off the still, watching the roiling liquid through the porthole, inhaling the aromatic steam, tasting the warm distillate as it trickled out at the end, listening to the distiller's insights about the process. A treat for all the senses.

You may be more science-y than I am and know all about rectification and reflux and volatility and vacuum distillation.

But what if, hypothetically, you also are a non-scientist who doesn't know all those technical terms? Well, on the off chance that you're like me, and prefer things explained in bite-sized chunks . . . let's do that.

What is distillation?

First up: distillation doesn't make alcohol. Fermentation makes alcohol: that's when tiny yeast monsters eat sugars and spit out booze and bubbles. But distillation concentrates a fermented liquid to make that booze into what we call a spirit.

It's all about purifying: separating the parts we don't want from the parts we do want.

What we don't want:

- Any toxic chemical compounds.

- Any bad flavours from the botanicals.

- Any other undesirable flavours (e.g. sulphur, which the copper removes).

- Too much water (if gin were weak, it wouldn't be a spirit).

What we do want:

- Plenty of ethanol (the kind of alcohol we drink).
- Good flavours from the botanicals.

These things all evaporate at different temperatures – for example, ethanol boils at 78.2°C / 173°F and water at 100°C / 212°F – so clever distillers can separate them by putting a fermented liquid and a bunch of botanicals into a still and carefully applying heat.

At the right temperatures (79-90°C / 174-194°F), the precious ethanol and the flavour molecules from the botanicals turn into a vapour and are whisked up and away, leaving the extra water and less pleasant dregs behind. Then they show up at the end of the process as gin.

It seems like magic to me. But apparently it's science.

If they'd let us make gin in science class, I would have paid more attention.

Different kinds of stills

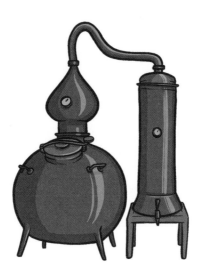

Pot still

- Barely changed in 500 years.

- Basically just a big kettle.

- Heats the liquid; vapours push through the pipe at the top then recondense into a liquid.

- Can carry lots of impurities across – bad for making neutral spirit.

- Carries lots of flavour across – good for making flavourful gin from neutral spirit and botanicals.

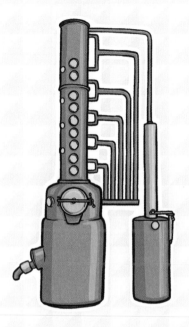

Column still

- Steampunk vibe; looks like a copper clarinet with submarine portholes.

- Does several distillations in one; vapours re-condense and re-vapourise over and over.

- Only the lightest and purest flavours make it into the final liquid.

- Produces cleaner spirits – excellent for making neutral spirit.

- Used by some gin makers to make super clean, smooth gin.

The gin-making process

If we tracked the gin-making process from grain to glass, we'd start with malting, brewing, fermenting, distilling to make neutral spirit . . .

But most gin makers start with neutral spirit and botanicals and get straight to re-distilling them together.

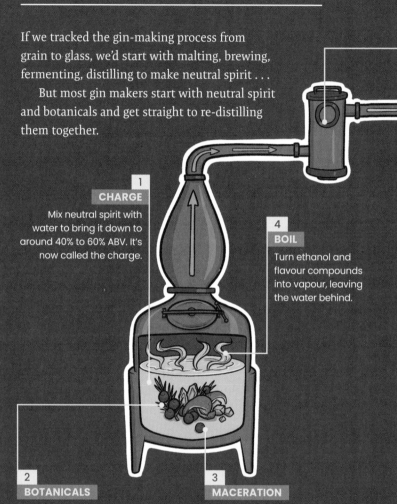

1
CHARGE

Mix neutral spirit with water to bring it down to around 40% to 60% ABV. It's now called the charge.

4
BOIL

Turn ethanol and flavour compounds into vapour, leaving the water behind.

2
BOTANICALS

The botanicals may be whole, or chopped/crushed/powdered. This affects how they release their flavour compounds.

3
MACERATION

Soak some or all of the botanicals in the spirit before distillation to draw out aromatic oils.

5
VAPOUR INFUSION

Put some or all of the botanicals in a gin basket. The vapour will pick up their aromatic oils on the way through.

6
CONDENSING

Send the vapour through pipes surrounded by cold water. The vapour cools and condenses into a liquid.

7
DISTILLATE

The distillate trickles into a receiving vessel over several hours. Gin makers separate the distillate into three parts: heads, hearts and tails. The hearts are the good stuff.

8
DILUTING

The hearts are full of booze and full of flavour, but too strong. Add water to bring the ABV down to the desired strength.

WE HAVE GIN!

It's ready to be bottled up, shipped out and drunk down. Unless it's going into a barrel – in that case, the journey continues . . .

What's best for the botanicals?

Boiling botanicals cooks them, changing the flavour over time. Vapour infusion leaves flavour compounds in their unaltered state. Most distillers use a mix of the two, boiling hardy botanicals and vapour infusing delicate botanicals.

Heads, hearts and tails

Not all of the distillate ends up as gin. The liquid trickling out keeps changing flavour and alcohol strength throughout the process; the stuff coming out at the beginning is very different to the stuff at the end.

The first part is the **heads**. You don't want to drink this bit. When you're re-distilling from neutral spirit, the heads aren't dangerous – the toxic compounds were stripped out when that base spirit was first distilled. But the heads pick up residual junk still in the pipes from the previous batch of gin.

The middle part is the **hearts**. When the distillate trickling out is tasting good, the distiller starts collecting it in a big vessel. They catch it early so they get as much ethanol and early flavour compounds as possible. They leave the hearts trickling as long as possible to keep bringing flavour from the botanicals. We like the hearts – they become our gin.

Eventually, we get to the **tails**. As the distillate keeps changing, it eventually contains minimal ethanol, less good flavour from the botanicals, and some undesirable flavours (think over-steeped tea, or over-extracted coffee). The distiller makes the cut – the hearts are now finished, and everything from here on out is the tails.

Building a flavour profile

To design a recipe, gin makers have to know how each botanical interacts with other botanicals, what form will work best for each (whole, chopped or powdered? Fresh or dried?), and how best to extract the flavour from each (maceration or vapour infusion?). They need to make sure delicate aromatic notes don't get lost, and intense notes don't overwhelm.

A one-dimensional gin would be boring; a good gin should have layers of flavour to hold your attention. Gin makers consider . . .

- **The top notes** – these are fresh and bright – think fruity, floral and herbal aromas. They're the first to rise up and hit you, but also the quickest to disappear.

- **The middle notes** – the complex array of flavours that hang around longer in the mouth and fill out the flavour profile. Often from spices, seeds and nuts.

- **The base notes** – the heavier compounds, often from roots, that stick around for a longer finish or aftertaste. You don't want a good gin to just vanish and be forgotten!

The end result of all this is a gin that holds together like an orchestral symphony.

Next time you're drinking a delicious gin, raise your glass to the skilled distiller who poured their heart and soul into it for your pleasure.

section two

Gin is gin, right? Right?!
Wrong. There's a lot of gin
out there – I mean a lot –
and more all the time. From
style to style, from distillery
to distillery, and even under
a gin maker's own roof,
there's huge variety in the
world of gin.

You'll just have to taste
all different gins in the
name of research. What
a gruelling task.

Types of gin

'Doesn't all gin taste the same?'

Whenever someone says this, I want to sit them down with 10 different gins covering a range of styles and let them taste the variety. I'd ramble about the history, ingredients and personalities of each style, but their tastebuds would educate them better than I ever could.

Until I strike it rich, I probably shouldn't go around buying 10 gins for complete strangers. But I can still ramble.

How strong is gin?

The legal definition of gin in the UK and EU says it must be at least 37.5% ABV to be labelled gin; in the USA, the minimum is 40% ABV. Gin makers think carefully about how strong they'll make their gin since it impacts the balance of flavours and aromas, which botanicals are highlighted or subdued, and even how the gin feels in your mouth.

Under 40% ABV – gins at this strength are generally designed to be cheaper, not better tasting.

Between 40% and 47% ABV – most gins around the world fall in here. This is a sweet spot for balancing the alcohol with the flavour of the botanicals.

Up to 54%, 57%, 60% ABV – fire the cannons! You're in navy strength territory. These gins bring potent booze and flavours. They're ideal for use in some kinds of cocktails.

London dry

If someone talks about 'the taste of gin', it's a London dry on their mind.

This is classic gin, and it's the most popular style in most gin-drinking parts of the world. It's interesting enough to hold up on its own, but straightforward enough to mix well with other drinks.

- **Hunting for a gin that displays the glory of juniper?**
  London dry.

- **Want to introduce someone to gin for the first time?**
  London dry.

- **Looking for a traditional gin to make G&Ts?**
  London dry.

- **Keen to make a classic martini or negroni?**
  London dry.

Origin

Today, we have access to so many high-quality gins that we take the clear botanical flavour profiles for granted. But gin wasn't always this clean.

Before 1830, the distillers around London were all using pot stills. The spirit they made was often rough and raw compared to gin today, full of off-flavours and other impurities. Gin makers did their best to cover these up by adding sweet botanicals and sugar with a heavy hand (see 'Old Tom' on page 83), and drinkers were happy enough.

Then along came the Coffey column still, and it was easier than ever before to produce a neutral spirit free from impurities and off-flavours. Game changer! This spirit was so clean, it didn't *need* to be loaded up with sweetener to be palatable. The juniper was allowed to shine through.

The other botanicals could be added with nuance and used to build a subtle and complex flavour profile.

Many distillers were based outside of London, but they knew the real money was in the city. They started to market gin like this as being 'dry' (as opposed to the lower-quality sweet gins), and the term 'dry' came to be used as shorthand for 'high quality' – exactly what the London gin crowd was after.

Thus the London dry style got its name.

What makes a London dry gin?

London dry gin doesn't have to be made in London, or anywhere near it – you'll find it produced all over the globe. There are official standards that qualify which gins can be called 'London dry', but if you're more interested in drinking the stuff than making it, here are the basics:

- **All the botanicals are distilled;** nothing is added after all the stages of distillation. (This means Hendrick's, which has cucumber and rose added after distillation, isn't a London dry.)

- **The predominant flavour** must be juniper.

- **It can't be coloured.** (Those beautiful purple butterfly pea flower gins? Not London dry.)

- **It must be dry.** (If there's more than 0.1 grams of sugars per litre, it's not London dry.)

Sometimes a gin will meet all these qualifications but won't say 'London dry' on the label. Maybe the distiller wants to emphasise the local provenance of their gin. Maybe they don't want to be associated with England. Maybe they're just short on label space.

What does it taste like?

At the risk of sounding stupid: London dry gin tastes like gin.

There's something delightfully straightforward about this style; think of the flavours weaving together like strands of a single rope. Juniper is there at the centre, but the other botanicals all play their part. Some highlight the piney, cedar character of juniper, while others pick up on its citrus notes. A good London dry is complex, but not complicated.

The dryness of this style creates an open space for the botanicals to leave their mark. But a London dry may not be completely dry – some botanicals like liquorice root can add a little sweetness to the flavour profile, and certain others (some citrus and flowers) can add the impression of sweetness.

If you're trying to familiarise yourself with gin, London dry is a good place to start before branching out into other styles. If you end up finding the pineyness of the juniper overwhelming, you can always sidestep to a citrussy contemporary gin and come back to a more assertive dry gin as your palate develops.

London dry is a classic for a reason. It's a no-brainer in a G&T. It goes well in a martini. It's versatile enough to use in most cocktails that call for gin. If you're going to have one gin in your bar at home, make it a London dry.

Plymouth

Talking about Plymouth gin as its own style always seems a bit silly to me, since it's just the one distillery making it. But when you've been making the same gin in the same distillery for over two hundred years, you've earned those bragging rights.

Origin

In 1700s London, cheap gin was to blame for drunkenness, toxic ingredients, crime waves and soaring death rates. As a result, gin's reputation was covered in . . . let's be polite and say 'mud'.

But when Black Friars Distillery was established in Plymouth in 1793, it managed to avoid that stink. Perhaps because it was 350 kilometres from the London slums that were the epicentre of the gin craze. Perhaps because Black Friars gin was a consistently high-quality product made in controlled factory conditions. Perhaps because Plymouth gin became a favourite of Royal Navy officers, who gave it a respectable name as they travelled the world. Or, hey, maybe the distillery had divine protection since it was a converted monastery.

Whatever the reason(s), Plymouth gin's reputation was shiny as a navy captain's gold-laced buttons. (Yes, I researched what kind of buttons they had.)

What makes a Plymouth gin?

Plymouth gin is made at the Plymouth Gin distillery. There used to be a UK law that said you couldn't call something 'Plymouth gin' unless it was made in Plymouth. But eventually everyone realised the term was protected by the brand's trademark anyway, so the law wasn't needed any more.

Plymouth gin is basically a subset of the London dry style; it meets all the requirements. But the balance of botanicals is distinctive, as it contains a higher proportion of orris and angelica root than your typical London dry, and more citrus peel.

What does it taste like?

Plymouth gin could still be described as juniper-forward, but it doesn't have the in-your-face pineyness you often get in a London dry. There's a move towards softer, earthier notes (from the roots) and more aromatic citrus (the lemon peel, orange peel, coriander and green cardamom all pull together on this). It goes down with ease.

Plenty of cocktail aficionados say the earthy softness and aromatic citrus of Plymouth make for the best dry martinis, and it was reportedly Winston Churchill's preferred gin.

Navy strength

Navy strength gin isn't just a vehicle for more booze; it's a style with an interesting history and an explosive balance of flavours. With its robust alcohol-to-botanical ratio, navy strength gin gives oomph to a G&T, tweaks the way ingredients interact in cocktails, and makes for a hefty drink on the rocks.

However you approach it, navy strength changes the rules of the game.

Origin

Britain conquered a quarter of the world on the strength of their navy. Their ships carried cannons and guns and gunpowder aplenty, as well as barrels of spirits in abundance to provide sailors with their daily allowance of grog.

Of course, it wouldn't do for a spilled barrel of gin to make the gunpowder unusable. How would a warship fend off pirates or attack helpless merchant ships?

To keep their stores of gunpowder safe (read: flammable), the British Navy carried spirits that were strong enough that even if they soaked the gunpowder, they wouldn't make it fizzle and fail. To test the strength of the spirits, they'd put a few grains of gunpowder into a glass of rum or gin and heat it with the old sun-through-a-magnifying glass trick. If it failed to ignite, the spirit was underproof. If it caught fire, they'd call it proof. If it exploded, it was overproof. (Please don't try this at home.)

Gin-soaked gunpowder isn't a live issue anymore, but in 1993, Plymouth Gin resurrected this old style of strong gin and marketed it as 'navy strength'. The new term spread like wildfire . . . or should I say it blew up like gunpowder?

What makes a navy strength gin?

There's no trademark on the term, and no legal standards for what can and can't be called 'navy strength'. But now that we measure alcohol without blowing stuff up (boring!), there's general agreement that any gin with an ABV of 57% or more can be called navy strength. You may see the odd English navy strength gin at

54.5% ABV, thanks to the confusing history of how the 'proof' rating changed over time.

It's simple for any distillery to make a navy strength version of their original gin; before bottling, they simply dilute their gin to 57% ABV (or higher) instead of the usual strength.

Alternatively, they can craft a new gin with a line-up of botanicals specifically designed to handle the brawny spirit.

What does it taste like?

There's no definition of what a navy strength gin 'should' taste like. You can get a navy strength London dry gin, or a more modern and experimental navy strength. Each has its own unique character.

But in all of them, the increased booze affects the way the flavours play out; a navy strength seems to turn down the volume of its botanicals (particularly the subtle and delicate flavours) as it turns up the volume of the alcohol warmth.

Comparing the taste of a distillery's flagship gin with their navy strength version is a fun experiment. Even more fun if you pull out a magnifying glass and some gunpowder. (Wait – no, I said not to do that.)

Navy strength gin works well in long drinks – the high alcohol punch stands up well, and the other (lower/no alcohol) ingredients draw out the botanicals. Or you can use navy strength gin to capture the historical accuracy of a cocktail created by the British Navy, like a gimlet or a pink gin.

Or just sip it on the rocks, like a strong whisky.

New world

Walk into a liquor store and browse the gin section. The majority of the gins there are either London dry or new world . . . but you may not see the words 'new world' on any labels.

'New western', 'new American', 'contemporary', 'new age' . . . these are all more or less referring to the same category. But you might not see these words, either.

New world gin isn't a style, exactly. It's a broad category, and it's loosely defined. People will disagree on precisely what it is, and what gins it includes.

If I had to describe it in six words? Dry gin that bends the rules.

Origin

Gin is supposed to taste like juniper first and foremost, right? That certainly used to be the case.

So when Bombay Sapphire came onto the scene in 1986, it was noteworthy that its juniper character was restrained and it had a stronger lemony-citrus bent than other gins at the time.

Then when Hendrick's hit the market in 1999 with its vibrant personality of rose and cucumber, it caused a stir.

Then Tanqueray No. 10 came out in 2000, bursting with three kinds of fresh whole citrus, and the juniper stood back and let it happen.

Some gin drinkers welcomed these innovations with open arms, while traditionalists harrumphed, eyebrows furrowed and moustaches aquiver. But the most interesting thing? People who thought they didn't like gin . . . liked *these* gins. From here, other distillers were emboldened to toy around with flavour profiles that allowed other botanicals to share the spotlight with juniper.

In 2009, ginsmith Ryan Magarian wrote an essay attempting to define this new style that many gins were now falling into (including his own Aviation). He coined the term 'new western dry' and discussed how each of these gins allows other botanicals to shine and shape the identity of the gin.

The explosion of craft distilleries in the United States pushed the growth of this new style of gin. But where the US led, distillers around the world followed, and now dry gins that don't fit the London dry category are widely available.

Many people don't love the term 'new western'. Personally, I prefer 'new world', channelling this line from Magarian's essay: 'I believe [Tanqueray No. 10 and Henrick's] have opened a door into *an entirely new world of flavor potential* for gin makers worldwide.'

What makes a new world gin?

New world is a nebulous term that you could apply to most contemporary gins that don't identify as another gin style. But these gins grew out of London dry: they're made in pretty much the same way; they're dry, but don't have to be bone dry; they can have a little sweetness, or the impression of sweetness from certain botanicals; and you can expect them to sit in the same ABV range.

Like I said, though: new world gin bends the rules.

Must it be clear? Nah.

Can it have things added after the final distillation? Yeah.

Officially, the juniper still needs to be 'dominant' for it to legally be called gin. (In the EU: 'the predominant flavour must be juniper'; in the USA: 'It shall derive its main characteristic flavour from juniper.') But I'm not the gin police, so: in a new world gin, the juniper may not be the leading botanical, and that's okay. In fact, it's kind of the point. Many new world gins are right on the edge of the legal definition of gin, with some dangling one foot over the edge. I won't snitch if you won't.

While it's still called new western or new American at times, this category definitely isn't localised to the States. New world gins are made all over the world.

That's one of the beautiful things about new world gin – distillers often use non-traditional botanicals from their region, and these ingredients give their gin a character you literally could not get somewhere else. A sense of place. It's why you'll see a gin labelled 'Mediterranean Gin', or 'Islay Dry Gin', or 'Australian Rainforest Gin'.

It's a brave new world.

What does it taste like?

What *doesn't* it taste like?

A new world gin tastes like a distiller's imagination. You have to get out there and explore them one sip at a time.

In America, plenty of gins go heavy on the coriander. Cardamom is becoming a bigger player. Lavender is common, which is notable considering how impactful it is; for a soft flower, it sure packs a punch. Then there are the distillers handpicking local herbs, flowers and fruits; a distiller in Texas and a distiller in Maine may both be making American gin, but the liquids could be worlds apart.

Lots of Australian gins look to native botanicals like finger lime, lemon myrtle, saltbush and Tasmanian pepperberry. Australia has bush, desert, rainforest and coast all in abundance, giving it a whopping great variety of plants to forage.

There's Spain's Gin Mare with its olives, basil, rosemary and thyme. There's Japan's Roku Gin with its cherry blossom, yuzu peel and green tea. There's Holland's Nolet's Gin with its peach, Turkish rose and raspberry.

The new world is your oyster. (Come to think of it, I've seen a few oyster gins, too.)

Old Tom

Sweetened gin originally existed as a way to fix bad gin, so Old Tom used to be an objectively lower quality beverage than London dry. Not anymore. Nowadays, Old Tom is about rounded flavours and retro cocktails.

Origin

This is the stuff that was popular in the 1700s, except it wasn't called Old Tom gin then. It was just called 'gin'.

Back then, most gin fit one of two categories: the gin made in distilleries with pot stills, which often showed flaws and impurities; and the nightmare liquid that people stirred up in back rooms. In both cases, you could improve the gin by adding strong flavours such as lemon and aniseed and sweet ingredients such as liquorice root. Or later – sugar.

Once distillers could make better quality gin in column stills, gin was divided into unsweetened (which became London dry) and sweetened (which became Old Tom). London dry won out, and Old Tom fell out of production in the early 20th century.

But the 21st century saw an interest in throwback cocktails. And if you want to make old-timey cocktails you need the right ingredients, including old-timey gin. That prompted modern distillers to bring back Old Tom so bartenders and drinkers could get that authentic flavour (minus the nastiness).

As for the name? There are a couple of theories.

- **Theory one:** a reference to a way illicit gin sellers would dodge liquor laws. They'd attach a wooden cat sign to their house and hide inside behind the sign. Customers would approach the wall from outside, put their coins in the cat's mouth, and receive a serve of gin delivered through a pipe under the cat's paw.

- **Theory two:** coined by Thomas Norris, who was apprenticed to distiller Thomas Chamberlain at Hodges Distillery. When young Tom struck out on his own to set up his own gin palace, one of the gins he sold was the old-fashioned, sweeter gin from his former employer. On these barrels, he'd write 'Old Tom's'.

What makes an Old Tom gin?

While London dry is about restraint and nuance, like the careful brushwork of someone painting a realistic portrait, Old Tom is like an impressionist painting – there's a willingness to play a little looser with the (botanical) brushstrokes.

Old Tom is lightly sweetened after distillation, and distillers work with the sugar to boost the botanical flavours. The sugar also gives the liquid a rounded feel in the mouth – think soft and smooth and silky.

What does it taste like?

Historically, Old Tom is sort of a bridge between genever and dry gin. But flavour-wise . . . well, it's kind of a bridge between genever and dry gin. It's drier than the malty genevers before it, and sweeter than London dry.

But don't expect syrupy stickiness. Old Tom gins are sweet compared to London dry, but they're not full of sugar. Some contain just enough to boost the mouthfeel but keep the sweetness to a minimum.

It's common for the non-juniper botanicals to lift their voices, so you may get citrus or liquorice flavours singing a little louder.

A tall, fizzy Tom Collins is *the* Old Tom cocktail, and is refreshing as all get-out. But there are a number of historical cocktails that factor in the sweeter flavour of Old Tom, like some of the earlier recipes for the martinez.

Since Old Tom is a bit more cuddly than London dry, some people enjoy it neat or on ice.

Genever

Some people talk about genever like it's the Neanderthal of gin – just a stage in gin's evolution. But while gin branched off from genever and became popular around the world, genever remains a spirit in its own right.

It's worth mentioning, though, since it's gin's cousin. Or perhaps it's the fun auntie who's always got a dirty joke to share at the family reunion.

Origin

Genever is old. There are spotty references to grape-based spirits infused with juniper from the 1300s, and in the 1500s, Dutch and Belgian distillers were making grain-based spirit infused with botanicals including juniper and calling it *jenever*.

During the Eighty Years War, British and Dutch soldiers fought side by side. And though they were from different countries, everyone drinks in the same language. The Brits fell in love with genever, and the drink made its way back to England. It grew in popularity, especially after William III – Dutch by birth – became King of England. Genever evolved into what we'd call gin, and genever proper fell out of fashion in England during the 18th century.

Back on the continent, genever continued to thrive . . . until the 20th century arrived. The First World War saw distilleries melted down by the Germans to make shell casings, and access to raw ingredients was limited. Then there was Prohibition in Belgium. And the Second World War.

Genever was all but snuffed out, but it's experienced a revival since the turn of the millennium. It's still young at heart.

What makes a genever?

People often say genever is like a hybrid between gin and whisky; Bols calls it 'the missing link between whisk(e)y and gin'.

It's a blend of two base spirits: one is neutral spirit; the other is malt wine, which is essentially an un-aged whisky. One or both of these is infused and distilled with botanicals, including juniper.

Jonge genever is the younger (more modern) style, with less than 15% malt wine in the mix. It's usually clear.

Oude genever is the older, more traditional stuff, with minimum 15% malt wine (often much more) and a light golden colour. Many oude genevers are aged in barrels.

If you see *moutwijn*, that's grandaddy genever – 100% malt wine, and closer to what genever was like back at the beginning.

EU specifications state that a spirit can only be called genever/jenever/genièvre if it's produced in the Netherlands, Belgium, or select areas of Germany and France.

What does it taste like?

Genever has layers of flavour: I could describe the maltiness of a blended scotch whisky, the round smoothness of oak, the combination of grain flavours, the herbal and spice tones of the gin-like botanicals . . .

. . . and I've also seen it described as 'elegant moonshine'. Take your pick.

Imagining a mix of gin and whisky may be a slight oversimplification, but it's as good a place to start as any.

Jonge genever is cleaner and less intensely flavoured, while oude genever is more about the botanicals and the malt character. If it's been aged in a barrel, it'll have character from the wood as well.

The layered nature of genever invites you to drink it neat or on the rocks. Or if you're actually in the Netherlands, ask for a *kopstootje* at the bar.

Some older cocktails that are now made with gin may have been invented when genever was the dominant spirit. Try a John Collins or a martinez with genever – you'll find them more complex than their gin-based counterparts.

A little headbutt

Ask a bartender in the Netherlands for a little headbutt – a *kopstootje* – and they'll serve you up a genever and a beer. It's a traditional way to enjoy the Dutch spirit.

It starts with a small tulip-shaped glass full of cold genever. I mean *full* – in danger of overflowing.

While the glass is sitting on the bar or table, bow down and take a sip. No using your hands! This is the 'little headbutt'.

Now that you're safe from spilling your drink, pick up the glass and toast. Some people shoot the genever then chase it with the beer, but you can drink them however you like.

Cask-aged

Is cask-aged gin a new style or an old one? After all, people were putting gin into wooden barrels hundreds of years ago.

But that wasn't a 'style' of gin. That was just gin. Nowadays, distillers pay special attention to what kind of barrels they're using, and they're particular about where they age the gin and for how long.

An old technique? A modern innovation? Let's just say 'what's old is new' and enjoy our drink.

Origin

Back in ye olde days, gin was shipped in wooden casks, stored in wooden casks, served from wooden casks. Before the UK's Single Bottle Act of 1861, you couldn't even buy gin in a bottle for take-away.

Over time, there was a shift away from wood as gin became more familiar with stainless steel, glass and plastic – sometimes because they were cost effective, sometimes because they treated the gin better.

Fast forward to 2008, when by coincidence two barrel-aged gins hit the market from opposite sides of the Atlantic: in the US, Ransom Old Tom, and in France, Citadelle Réserve.

They were the product of the same thought experiment: 'Gin used to be shipped in wooden barrels. How might that impact the flavour?' (Though Citadelle's distiller probably had the thought in French.)

Amid the cocktail frenzy of the 2000s, they were a hit. Soon other craft distilleries jumped on board, too – many of them were waiting for whisky to age, so why not age some gin in the meantime as well?

What started as an attempt to recreate a historically accurate flavour has evolved into a technique and style of its own.

What makes a cask-aged gin?

In short? Take some gin and stick it in a barrel for a while.

Unlike whisky, gin doesn't have strict rules around ageing. A few weeks? A few months? A year? Anything goes.

Distillers can use new casks or old casks. Oak is the most popular option, but gin makers can use any barrels. I've seen a distiller age their juniper spirit in a juniper wood barrel. Juniperception!

In America, gin can't legally be called 'barrel-aged', so distilleries get creative with their labelling, using terms like oak-rested, cask-finished, barrelled, reserve and antique.

What does it taste like?

First, appreciate its colour. While London dry gin is perfectly clear, barrel-aged gins range from pale gold like white wine, to darker brown like whisky, to winey red. Delightful.

Now, to the taste.

Gin rested in a new cask has a brighter, more assertive wood character – perhaps honey, vanilla or coconut notes. Old wood gives softer, more layered character – a patina of flavour. Used barrels will lend colour and flavour from the wine or spirit that was previously housed in the barrel, such as bourbon or sherry.

Some of gin's aromatic oils can be lost in the ageing process, and lighter flavours can be overshadowed while heavier juniper and coriander notes can sharpen up. But good distillers know what they're doing, choosing their barrels carefully and deciding when the gin has aged enough (longer isn't always better).

To fully appreciate the depth of character that ageing gives a gin, try tasting one of these gins neat or on the rocks before mixing it with anything.

But the intriguing personality of a cask-aged gin – whether it be spicy, smoky or boozy – also lends itself to complex cocktails. A negroni with an extra facet? A manhattan with bourbon barrel-aged gin in place of bourbon? A barrel-aged gin old fashioned? All you need is an overstuffed armchair and you're in for a great evening.

Sloe gin

One look at this ruby sipper and you'll say, 'Toto, I've a feeling we're not in London anymore.'

Forget what you know about 'normal gin' – this a sweet liqueur. It isn't clear, it isn't dry, and it isn't juniper forward. And its history doesn't look to crowded London, but to the green sprawl of pastoral England.

Origin

I've always loved the romantic notion of wandering the English countryside and picking berries from hedges. This is the world where sloe gin was born.

As the 1700s ticked on, Britain saw cheaper gin than ever before (much of it poor quality), cheaper sugar than ever before (from slave plantations in the West Indies), and abundant sloe berries (from the blackthorn hedges used to separate new private farms across the land). The gin tasted nasty and the sloes were tart and astringent, but bring them together with sugar and what do you have? Delicious sloe gin!

Traditionally, farmers' wives (the real heroes here) would prick each sloe with a thorn from the hedge and soak the fruits in gin with plenty of sugar. Over months, the flavour and colour would leak into the gin, making a deep red liquid. They'd strain the liquid off and have sloe gin, while the boozy fruit left over could be eaten or turned into jam. (Note to self: find sloe gin jam and slather it on chunky bread.)

What makes a sloe gin?

Sloe gin's a bit sneaky. Technically it's a liqueur, not a true gin, usually clocking in between 15% and 30% ABV. But it's got a note from its mum that says it's allowed to be labelled as gin. (European regulations give sloe gin a special pass as long as it's above 25% ABV.)

Most commercial sloe gin still uses the same basic method as the farmer's wives of the past, steeping wild fruit in gin with or without sugar. But there are more efficient ways to get the flavour out than poking a thorn into each and every fruit. (Who would've thunk it?) Freezing the berries ruptures the cells in the fruit so the natural sugars and flavours can escape easily, making the reddish-purple booze we love.

Sometimes distillers will riff on the idea of sloe gin, using fruits like the Australian Davidson plum.

What does it taste like?

It's sweet and sticky, with a slightly tart and bitter balance. The gin brings background complexity, but the dominant flavour here is the sloes themselves – notes of plum, sour cherry, cranberry, pomegranate. If the maker was patient, the alcohol will have pulled some flavour from the stone of the sloe as well as the flesh, adding an aromatic almond-like character.

You'll occasionally find a sloe gin at full strength (over 37.5% ABV), with more botanical balance sitting alongside the sloe.

In winter: sip this liqueur neat after dinner as you would a nice port, or bring it together with spices and make a warm mulled drink.

In summer: lengthen sloe gin with soda water for vibrant refreshment, or use it in a cocktail. The sloe gin fizz is a classic, or you can sub out some of the London dry in a bramble.

Gin liqueur

If you've got a sweet tooth, find yourself some gin liqueurs.

While sloe gin is a style of its own, 'gin liqueur' is a catch-all term for drinks made in a similar way – by steeping fruits or other ingredients in gin to make a lower-alcohol, sweeter beverage. They're usually sold in pretty bottles and make for a perfect gift to buy for someone in your life – especially if you can get that someone to invite you over for a drink.

Origin

Nowadays, we think of liqueurs as cute and fancy. But they came into being as a way to help miserable poor people get drunk. At a time when most gin tasted like paint stripper, adding fruit and sugar covered up the horrid flavour.

Over time, gin got better and economic conditions improved for many people, and producers made gin liqueurs simply because they were delicious drinks.

What makes a gin liqueur?

Gin liqueurs are lower in alcohol than gin, hovering between 15% and 30% ABV (though as with sloe gin, you may find some exceptions with higher alcohol). They're sweet and boldly flavoured.

Distillers can make gin liqueurs with basically anything. Citrus, figs, rhubarb, rose, chocolate, gingerbread . . . it's all up for grabs.

What does it taste like?

Most gin liqueurs have a specific fruit or other flavour that overtakes the juniper and other botanicals. They mostly taste like a sweet syrup of the labelled flavour – they're not aiming for subtlety – but with a boozy warmth and an undercurrent of gin complexity.

However, some gin liqueurs are simply made with the same botanicals as the gin, with no other flavours added. Here you can taste juniper, citrus and other ginny notes with a lighter,

sweeter flavour and more syrupy mouthfeel. It's like drinking a cartoon version of gin.

Drink a gin liqueur neat, over ice, or as a spritz topped up with sparkling wine or soda water. Or just pour a shot over a scoop of vanilla ice cream. Your mum isn't watching.

Specialty

I almost called this category 'crazy flavours', but landed on 'specialty' in the end. These gins don't fit into any of the other categories, and they certainly don't fit the mould of traditional dry gin.

Origins

People have been adding things to change the flavour of gin for hundreds of years.

When gin began its resurgence in the 2000s, some distillers started messing around with flavours to add new gins to their repertoire. They added certain botanicals with a heavy hand, or experimented with adding different fruits or other ingredients that would take the flavour of a gin in a whole new direction.

While I applaud their creativity and innovation, they're really just continuing a centuries-old trend of adding stuff to gin. The return of boldly flavoured and coloured gins was inevitable. And today's ginsmiths can carry the torch even further since they have access to far more ingredients and processes than anyone before them.

What makes a specialty gin?

Whether they're labelled as flavoured gins, fruit-infused gins, spiced gins or something else, these are gins with flavours that are happy to overshadow the juniper. While some *may* just about fit in the new world category, most go well beyond it.

New world gins may paint flames on the side of your car, but specialty gins pimp out the whole vehicle, adding a body kit and neon lights and bouncing down the road blasting doof-doof music.

New world gins shift the balance to favour certain botanicals; specialty gins are purposely unbalanced, with a whole new identity.

Blackberry gin. Chocolate gin. Coffee gin. Shiraz gin.

Some people reckon these are barely gins at all, and maybe shouldn't even be allowed to use the word 'gin'. But I'm not too bothered. I say bring on the crazy flavours – especially if they entice more people to step into the world of gin.

What does it taste like?

Depends on the gin, of course!

The one thing they have in common is that they taste like what they say on the label. Like gin liqueurs, these flavour grenades aren't aiming for subtlety. Distillers add plenty of their chief ingredient, whether that be fruit, spices, flowers, whatever, and that's the first thing you'll taste.

But unlike, say, flavoured vodka, you should still be able to taste something other than the title ingredients – gin. Gin is the base drink, and juniper and other botanicals should still pull their weight and contribute to the flavour profile, even if it's only as undertones.

Four Pillars Bloody Shiraz is a bloody good drop, and has inspired a string of shiraz gins in Australia. It takes eight weeks for the shiraz wine grapes steeped in dry gin to release their glory, but pour some Bloody Shiraz into a glass with a splash of soda water and it'll be lucky to last eight minutes.

I've had a gingerbread gin and a Christmas pudding gin; both are perfect for warming your soul by a crackling fire.

The Amalfi Coast is known for its vibrant colours and zesty citrus, and Italy's Malfy Gin captures both. This brand takes the idea of a citrussy gin to a whole new level. Their Con Arancia ('with orange') is a guilty pleasure of mine.

Notable gin brands

Certain gins can be found in bars and bottle shops around the world. Some are older than the Eiffel Tower and the US Constitution, and others are charismatic newcomers that haven't wasted any time leaving their mark. It's worth getting familiar with a handful of them.

Think of the following pages as online dating profiles for some of the notable gins out there. If you see one that catches your eye, perhaps reach out and get to know it a little better. Who knows where it'll lead? You may meet the love of your life.

Gordon's

Place of origin: London, England
Year established: 1769
Flagship gin: Gordon's London Dry
Also known for: a variety of fruity gins, including Gordon's Pink with strawberries, raspberries and redcurrants.
A little about Gordon's: Gordon's is all but synonymous with gin, being one of the oldest gin brands in the world.

Founder Alexander Gordon was a pioneer of the dry gin style; at a time when others were making rough gin and covering the impurities with sugar, Gordon's was well crafted with no sugar needed. That was over 250 years ago, and Gordon's flagship gin has been distilled continuously to the same recipe ever since. You don't last that long unless you're doing something right.

The green glass bottle of Gordon's London Dry, which is iconic in its home country, is virtually unknown in the rest of the world; the exported versions are in clear glass bottles with a yellow and red label.

Gordon's is sold at different strengths around the world, ranging from 37% to 47.3% ABV. Try to find one of the stronger versions if you can; the ones under 40% ABV don't have the same oomph or botanical balance.

Tanqueray

Place of origin: London, England
Year established: 1830
Flagship gin: Tanqueray London Dry
Also known for: Tanqueray No. 10, which builds on the original four botanicals of Tanqueray London Dry with chamomile and three kinds of fresh whole citrus – grapefruit, orange and lime.

A little about Tanqueray: Tanqueray's London Dry remains the same as the product that was created in 1830.

Gordon's and Tanqueray merged in 1898 to build an unbeatable alliance in a competitive gin market (and remain stablemates to this day), but each brand retained its distinct identity. Today,

Gordon's is the number one gin in the UK, while Tanqueray is one of the biggest sellers in the US. Way to conquer the world, guys.

In 1933, President Roosevelt sipped a historically significant Tanqueray gin and tonic to officially mark the end of Prohibition.

After Prohibition, the Depression and a couple of world wars, when America was ready to continue its love affair with cocktails, Tanqueray released its signature green cocktail shaker bottle in 1948.

In 1964, sales of Tanqueray doubled in the US after the Rat Pack were spotted ordering Tanqueray martinis in a club in San Francisco.

Beefeater

Place of origin: London, England
Year established: 1863
Flagship gin: Beefeater London Dry
Also known for: Beefeater 24 is the brand's premium gin, adding Japanese sencha, Chinese green tea and grapefruit peel to the botanical line-up. Burrough's Reserve is rested in red and white Bordeaux oak casks.

A little about Beefeater: the company's founder bought a distillery in 1863 and started his company 'James Burrough, Distiller and Importer of Foreign Liqueurs'. (Catchy, right?) He added Beefeater gin to his repertoire in 1876, and it quickly became the brand's flagship product.

While Gordon's and Tanqueray have both shifted their UK production to Scotland, Beefeater is still produced in the heart of Old London Town. I suppose the distillery needs to stick close to its namesakes – the Yeoman Warders in the funny red outfits who guard the Crown Jewels.

Bombay

Place of origin: New York City (NY), USA / Cheshire, England
Year established: 1960
Flagship gin: Bombay Sapphire
Also known for: Star of Bombay, which adds ambrette seeds and bergamot orange peel to the Bombay Sapphire line-up.

A little about Bombay: made in England and named after a city in India – who'd have guessed Bombay Gin originated in New York? But that's where a lawyer named Allan Subin came up with the idea in 1957 to bring a new gin brand to the American market.

He contracted production to G&J Greenall's in England, where Bombay Gin was made from their original 1761 recipe. Unlike most gins, Bombay uses vapour infusion for all of its botanicals.

While Bombay Gin came out in 1960 – and did very well – it was Bombay's premium release in 1986 that changed the game. At a time when gin's popularity was low and cocktails were just becoming cool again, Bombay Sapphire entered in a gleaming blue bottle, saying, 'I'm glam, but I'm for everyone. I'm British, but I'm exotic.'

Bombay Sapphire proudly imports spices from warm countries around the world: from Chinese liquorice to Moroccan coriander seeds to West African grains of paradise.

As of 2013, Bombay Sapphire has its own distillery home – Laverstoke Mill in Hampshire.

Hendrick's

Place of origin: Girvan, Scotland
Year established: 1999
Flagship gin: Hendrick's Original. It has a contemporary botanical line-up, and is infused with Bulgarian rose and cucumber after distillation.
Also known for: Hendrick's has a rotating range of gins with outlandish botanicals.

A little about Hendrick's: a pioneer of modern gin with an old timey aesthetic. Hendrick's emerged with an approach to flavour unlike existing gin brands and brought a new flavour to the gin world. Since two antique stills were used in production, a clever marketer built the distinctive branding around Victorian-era whimsy (or is it Edwardian? I don't know my old monarchs). The gins come in apothecary-style medicine bottles, and are referred to as 'concoctions'.

Hendrick's Original is still made with the recipe master distiller Lesley Gracie developed in the '90s. Inside her laboratory is her 'Cabinet of Curiosities', which contains a flavour library of essential oils, distillates, extracts and botanicals. She tends to a greenhouse full of Mediterranean plants and another full of tropical plants – all in the name of experimenting with botanicals from around the world.

Plymouth

Place of origin: Plymouth, England
Year established: 1793
Flagship gin: Plymouth Original
Also known for: Plymouth Navy Strength – this is the brand that resurrected and named the style in 1993.
A little about Plymouth: Plymouth Gin (the company) is the only distillery in the world that makes Plymouth gin (the style).

Plymouth Original has been produced to the same recipe on the same site since the distillery opened in 1793. I hope you're as impressed as I am by that.

Originally the site was a monastery, which is why the bottles still have 'Black Friars Distillery' embossed on them today.

Ginebra San Miguel

Place of origin: Manila, Philippines
Year established: 1834
Flagship gin: Ginebra San Miguel
A little about Ginebra San Miguel: unless you've been to the Philippines or you're a gin nerd, you may not have heard of GSM. But it rates a mention because it's consistently the top-selling gin in the world, outselling the next top brand by at least five times!

You see, the Philippines accounts for about a third of the world's gin consumption . . . and most of that is Ginebra San Miguel. It's cheap (litre for litre, about the same price as beer). The company has huge advertising spend. And it's embedded itself into the Filipino culture of hospitality.

You don't need to go chase down a bottle of this. But how could I not tell you about the biggest selling gin in the world?

The Botanist

Place of origin: Bruichladdich, Scotland
Year established: 2011
Flagship gin: The Botanist Islay Dry Gin, which has a whopping 31 botanicals – nine traditional and 22 hand-foraged on the island of Islay itself. (Actually, the juniper is foraged on the island as well.)
A little about The Botanist: the Bruichladdich Distillery has been making whisky since 1881, but it wasn't until 2011 that they gifted the world with The Botanist gin. While Islay scotch whisky is known for flavours of peat and smoke, you won't find any of that in The Botanist – just the botanicals doing their thing. The gorgeous bottle features the Latin names of the botanicals imprinted in raised letters on the glass.

The Islay botanicals are foraged by retired botanists Richard and Mavis Gulliver, who head to the hills, into the peat bogs and along the coastal shores to pick the botanicals. If you ask me, that sounds like a bloody amazing way to spend one's 'retirement'.

Roku

Place of origin: Osaka, Japan
Year established: 2017
Flagship gin: Roku, which uses eight traditional botanicals and six Japanese botanicals.
A little about Roku: Roku has quickly found its place in bars around the world as a Japanese craft gin, though its parent company Suntory has been in the booze business since 1899.

It's a distinctly Japanese spirit. 'Roku' means 'six' in Japanese, and its unique hexagonal bottle represents its six Japanese botanicals: sanshō peppercorns and yuzu peel give an aroma of spicy citrus to the nose; sakura flowers and leaves bring the essence of cherry blossom to bear; two kinds of green tea make themselves known throughout. Each botanical is distilled separately by whatever technique is best suited for extracting its particular flavours.

Four Pillars

Place of origin: Healesville, Australia
Year established: 2013
Flagship gin: Four Pillars Rare Dry Gin, containing whole fresh citrus, Chinese spices and Australian native botanicals.
Also known for: Four Pillars' greatest contribution to the global gin scene has to be their world-first

Bloody Shiraz, made by steeping shiraz (syrah) grapes from the Yarra Valley wine region.

A little about Four Pillars: six years. That's how long it took Four Pillars to go from being founded to winning International Gin Producer of the Year at the International Wine & Spirit Competition. Then they did it again the following year.

In addition to their flagship gin, Four Pillars makes all kinds of experimental gins – some aged in sherry casks or chardonnay barrels; some soaked with surprising citrus like yuzu or cumquats; some out of left field like Olive Leaf Gin made with olive leaf tea and olive oil, or their seasonal Christmas pudding infused gin. They also make non-alcoholic versions of their Rare Dry Gin and their Bloody Shiraz.

Aviation

Place of origin: Portland (OR), USA
Year established: 2006
Flagship gin: Aviation American Gin, a modern gin that shows off floral lavender and earthy spice, and touches upon root beer.
Also known for: its association with actor Ryan Reynolds, who was a part-owner for a couple of years and remains an ambassador for the brand.

A little about Aviation: one of the brand's founders, Ryan Magarian, wrote an essay in 2009 to define the new category of gin that Aviation sat within; he named it 'new western dry' (see 'New world' on page 79).

But to many, Aviation is best known for being 'Ryan Reynolds' gin'. Even though Aviation has since sold to beverage giant Diageo (a multinational company, not a literal giant), Reynolds still promotes Aviation in ads, on his social media and in a number of his films. And since he's roguishly handsome, has a dry sense of humour and wears cool jackets, he does it well.

Aviation Gin is named for the aviation cocktail, popular through the 1920s and '30s, and the gin's flask-like art deco bottle is a nod to that time period.

Seagram's

Place of origin: Lawrenceburg (IN), USA
Year established: 1939
Flagship gin: Seagram's Extra Dry. It's known for its unique bumpy glass bottle.
A little about Seagram's: Seagram's is the largest selling gin in the USA, and has been for decades. The brand's strong American messaging is quiet about the fact that Seagram's originated as a Canadian company in the mid-1800s. But the gin has never been produced anywhere outside the USA.

While Seagram's isn't labelled as a cask-rested gin, it actually spends a few weeks in barrels.

If you're a fan of '90s hip hop, here's your Friday night: listen to Snoop Dogg's 1994 hit 'Gin and Juice' and mix yourself a drink of the same name. While one of the verses reveals that Dr Dre is a Tanqueray guy, it appears Ol' Snoopy looked to Seagram's as his gin of choice, as immortalised in his poetry:

'Now that I got me some Seagram's gin,
Everybody got they cups, but they ain't chipped in.'

I must say, I hope that as Mr Dogg grew in fame and acquired more wealth, he also grew in generosity and was happy to share his gin with his acquaintances – even those who didn't chip in.

Bols

Place of origin: Amsterdam, The Netherlands
Year established: 1575(!)
Flagship gin: Bols Genever Original, which is not gin. It's genever, made according to a Bols recipe from 1820.
A little about Bols: Bols claims to be the oldest distillery brand in the world, and as they're approaching half a millennium, I'm not sure who'd argue with them. Someone really old, I guess.

The distillery started in 1575 by making liqueurs and launched its first genever in 1664. By the end of that century, Bols was an international brand, exporting genever and hundreds of liqueurs around the world. Nowadays, those at Bols still refer to a handbook compiled by one of the owners in 1830, which lends credence to their motto *Semper Idem* – 'Always the same.'

But this isn't a stagnant company – they keep pace with evolving cocktail culture. Any visitor to Amsterdam should visit the

House of Bols to do the cocktail experience at their museum. The science! The smells! The vibrating room! And of course: the sipping.

Bols makes gin as well, but they're known for their genever, so give it a try.

Come on. Grab life by the Bols.

Sipsmith

Place of origin: London, England
Year established: 2009
Flagship gin: London Dry Gin
Also known for: the wittily named V.J.O.P. Gin (Very Junipery Over Proof) is Sipsmith's navy strength.
A little about Sipsmith: to stem the flow of (cheap, nasty and excessive) gin in London during the dangerous Gin Craze, the Gin Act of 1751 stopped people producing gin in stills with a capacity under 1800 litres. This rule was much needed at the time, putting gin production back in the hands of 'respectable' businesses. But 250 years later, it was simply a nuisance that prohibited small batch gin in the UK. Sipsmith's founders claim the credit for pushing through this law in 2009, and

they opened the first copper pot distillery in London in a couple of centuries. You can thank them (and their 300 litre still named Prudence) for enabling the rise of craft gin in the UK.

Sipsmith's branding is London to the core – it buys its suits on Savile Row, and secretly loves Harrods. Its flagship gin isn't one of these newfangled new world gins – it's closer to the platonic ideal of a London dry. Even its more experimental drops drip Britishness. Lemon drizzle cake? Terry's Chocolate Orange? Pimm's cup? Sipsmith has a bottle reminiscent of each.

section three

Does anyone really need advice on how to drink gin? The G&T is one of the easiest drinks to make, and it's even easier to drink.

But what if I told you you could enjoy gin even more? Because there may not be many wrong ways to drink gin . . . but some ways of drinking gin are very right.

Tasting gin

When you're drinking something like a well-made gin and tonic, it should delight all five senses: see the colourful fruit and herb garnishes, feel the cool condensation on a slick highball glass, hear the bubbles popping and fizzing and the ice clinking, smell the sharp punch of pine and peppercorns, taste the union of botanicals from across continents and the bittersweet bite of tonic water.

But we're going to put that aside for the moment and talk about tasting gin on its own: thoughtfully, with no ice or mixer, at room temperature.

Before you slam the book shut, hear me out. Even if you have no desire to taste gin neat, there are benefits to this.

It helps you articulate what you like and don't like.

It helps you understand 'gin words', which pays off when you read labels or order at a bar.

It helps you distinguish the differences between gins. This can help you get an idea of whether you'll like a gin even before you've tasted it, and to figure out which gins you prefer with tonic and in different cocktails.

And it really is an enjoyable activity.

You don't need any special skills or experience to do this; just the willingness to stop and notice. To pay attention to what you're drinking.

Trust me. It's worth it.

Getting ready

Environment – no heavy perfume or spicy curry smells in the air.

Glass – Glencairn glasses are perfect for this. Otherwise, a curvy red wine glass is a good replacement, or a rocks glass will suffice.

Gins – a few different gins from the same distillery? A few of the same style? A few sharing similar botanicals? Or a few completely different gins? Keep it to three or four gins to avoid palate fatigue, and taste them in order of lowest to highest ABV.

Pour size – a little goes a long way – 15 ml (½ fl oz) or less of each gin is enough for tasting. That also leaves you room to come back and try them a few ways.

Taste the gin blind first – no blindfold necessary. Just avoid reading about the flavours and botanicals on the label or distiller's website before you taste. It'll help you sharpen your palate.

Smell

Give smell the attention it deserves. The aroma of gin isn't just an added bonus, but an important part of the flavour profile. When you smell gin, aromatic molecules from the gin go up your nostrils and hit your sensory receptors; your brain then interprets these and you get smells. When you sip gin, these aroma molecules enter your nose via the back of your mouth, and help shape the overall flavour that way. I suppose you could call it mouth-smell. Or nose-flavour. Either way, it's a pretty cool system!

The upshot of all this? Smelling your gin is a significant part of the tasting process.

Give your gin a swirl. Swirling your gin for a few seconds gets some oxygen in there, which helps to wrangle those aromatics and bring them up to the mouth of the glass.

The exception here is navy strength gin. Its alcohol fumes can be full-on, so you don't need to agitate them even more.

Give it a sniff. Carefully! The alcohol fumes can all gather and concentrate at the top of the glass, so if you do a huge sniff at the beginning, those fumes will rush up your nostrils and burn your nose. It's not pleasant.

Some people blow the alcohol fumes away before sniffing, or waft the glass under their nose and sniff the air above.

My technique is different, but I've found it to be super effective.

The secret? Mouth-smelling.

I hold the glass up to my nose, but instead of inhaling through my nose (the way we normally sniff), I inhale through my mouth. It sounds strange. It looks funny. But 'smelling' like this picks up the aromas of the gin without getting the alcohol burn. Score a point for the mouthbreathers!

Give it a think. What's your first impression of the aroma? The first things you smell are the most volatile aromatics, referred to as the top notes. They smell strong at the beginning, but they may fade soon. Bright citrus and floral notes are common here, and some aspects of juniper.

But the aroma of gin isn't one dimensional, and it doesn't all come at once. You know how when you meet a new person, they make a first impression on you, but more of their character and personality reveals itself as you get to know them? The same is true of gin – different elements of the aroma reveal themselves after a while, as the middle notes and base notes show up.

Keep smelling. What new aromas are there? Other fruits? Herbs? Spices? Sweetness? Wood? Earthiness? Can you pick out individual botanicals?

Give it a second between sniffs. Smelling different gins can get confusing. Go easy on your poor little nose.

You can 'reset' your sense of smell in between gins, or even between sniffs of the same gin. Smell some coffee beans to cleanse your olfactory sense, or even just sniff the back of your hand or the inside of your elbow. This is a neutral smell (to you), and gives your nose a fresh start.

Taste

Take a sip. Finally! How have we gone this long without actually drinking any gin?!

Start with a tiny sip, like when your cup of coffee is too hot to drink.

You have tastebuds all over your tongue, so make sure you put them all to work. Move the liquid around in your mouth and get it to touch all parts of your tongue – front, sides and back.

Let the gin sit in your mouth for a few seconds before you swallow. This gives your taste receptors time to process the flavours and communicate them to your brain.

As a bonus, you'll be mouth-smelling the gin this whole time, too.

Take a breath. Getting more oxygen to mingle with the spirit can help you detect and identify flavours. Suck in some air while holding the gin in your mouth, or you can copy those wine experts who slurp their wine. Anything wine can do, gin can do better!

Take notice. Does it taste sweet or dry? Does it taste simple (one dominant flavour) or complex? Does it taste similar to the aroma or quite different?

As the gin sits in your mouth, try to identify the individual flavours. Just like with the aroma, different flavours may come through at different times, transitioning from the beginning to the middle to the end of a sip, and different again with subsequent sips.

With beer and whisky and wine, you describe what the flavours taste *similar* to (e.g. 'this merlot tastes *like* plum'). With gin, you're often picking out the flavours of actual botanicals in the gin.

Trying to put your finger on individual botanicals is fun . . . but it's not easy. Some are subtle, or don't come through distinctly. Some are unfamiliar because of the way the flavours were extracted, or the way they interact with other botanicals. And some are ingredients we're not very familiar with in the first place.

So don't worry if you have difficulty. You can always take another sip. (Until the gin is all gone, that is.)

Keep calm and carry on.

Take a moment to consider the aftertaste. Just because you've swallowed the gin doesn't mean the gin is finished with you!

Just as you got a first impression of your gin, the aftertaste – also called the finish or the bottom note – will give you a lasting impression. One particular note may linger. The flavours may all merge together. Or the finish may not be the same as what's come before. Exhale the gin vapour after you've swallowed, and you might be surprised to taste something new in there.

Take notes. It's one thing to pause and think about what the gin tastes like, but you'll get the best results when you force yourself to put your thoughts into words and write those words down. The more you engage your mind when you drink, the more you'll notice the differences between gins, from the obvious to the nuanced. In other words: when you take notes, you get better at tasting gin.

You can write more than just what botanicals you tasted; take note of any impressions or associations you have with the gin. If three different gins all taste 'soapy' to you and you realise they're all heavy on lavender, you'll discover you have an association between lavender and soap.

As a bonus, you'll end up with a record of which gins you enjoyed and which ones you didn't. Look for patterns among the ones you love and find more like them!

Write it down

Here are some ideas of things to take note of . . .

What do you smell? (Beginning? Middle? End?)

What do you taste? (Beginning? Middle? End?)

What does this gin remind you of?

What do you like about it?

What don't you like about it?

Does one predominant botanical stand out, or are the flavours rounded and balanced?

How do you think it would go with tonic? With other mixers? In different cocktails?

Here's a guide to get you started and help you identify what you're smelling and tasting. Start broad (e.g. citrus, spice), then try to narrow in on more specific aromas and flavours (e.g. grapefruit, clove).

FLORAL

rose, violet, lavender, jasmine, hibiscus, honeysuckle, chamomile, elderflower

HERB

juniper, eucalyptus, thyme, sage, rosemary, basil, mint, fennel, lemongrass, lemon myrtle

FRUIT

berry, apple, rhubarb, cucumber, melon, cherry, apricot, pineapple, pear, grape

CITRUS

lemon, lime, orange, grapefruit, bergamot, mandarin, lemon peel, lime peel

NUTTY

almond, hazelnut, wattle seed, pistachio, macadamia

SWEET

honey, vanilla, dried fruit, tamarind, liquorice root

EARTHY

pine, cedar, wood, angelica root, orris root, green tea, Earl Grey tea, jasmine tea

SPICE

anise, cinnamon, coriander, pepper, clove, allspice, ginger, caraway, nutmeg, cardamom

Encyclopaedia botanica

Not sure of the difference between thyme and sage? Don't know what cardamom smells like? Haven't had grapefruit or mandarin in a long time? Never smelled jasmine before?

Make a list of botanicals you'd like to get more familiar with, and treat it as a scavenger hunt! Track them down to smell/taste, and over time you'll become a walking talking botanical database.

The next step

Once you've tasted the gin neat, it's time to open it up and see what new flavours will reveal themselves. I've tasted gins that are simple and citrussy when neat, but release their herbal notes with a few drops of water, and other gins that taste aniseed-y when neat, but like fairy floss when a splash of tonic water is introduced.

You can try adding the following:

- **A small amount of water** – dilutes the gin, which opens up the flavours.

- **An ice cube** – cools the gin, which can dial down the alcohol fumes and help some of the quieter botanicals to pop out.

- **A little soda water** – the carbonation adds vibrancy to the aromas and taste.

- **A little tonic water** – balances the alcohol with sweetness and bitterness.

- **If you're feeling particularly scientific,** you could even try the gin all four ways and compare them.

I usually go with a sprinkle of room temperature water – it's surprising, but water can unlock brand new aromas as it interacts with the alcohol and oils in the gin, and releases some of the subtle and delicate notes.

Congratulations! If you went through the whole tasting process, you've gained knowledge of a few specific gins, and you've also levelled up your tasting skills overall. You're well on your way to becoming a ginnoisseur.

Serving up your gin

The glass

It's just a cup, right? Pour your gin into a champagne flute or a Mickey Mouse coffee mug and it'll taste the same.

But the kind of glass you use *does* make a difference: the way it releases a drink's aroma into the air; the feel and weight of the glass in your hand; the way a certain glass makes you feel like Audrey Hepburn or Humphrey Bogart.

And never underestimate the visual appeal of a glass. Aesthetics matter.

Cocktails bars will have a specific glass for any drink they serve up. But choosing a glass shape isn't always about rules or tradition – many of us simply gravitate towards our favourite. I know I do.

Highball / Collins

These glasses are tall, versatile and high volume. They can be cylindrical or hold a slight bulge, plain and clear or patterned crystal. A highball has been the default shape for a gin and tonic for a long time. It's good for any long drink on a hot day.

(Technically, these are two different shapes of glass – a Collins is taller and narrower and holds more volume, and is the standard for serving a Tom Collins. But highballs and Collins glasses are often used interchangeably.)

Copa de balon

Sounds fancy, right? People refer to this as a Spanish balloon glass. But the literal translation is 'ball cup', which is much funnier.

This glass comes from Spain, where gin flows like a river and art infuses every corner of life, including beverages. A copa offers plenty of room for ice and several garnishes – perfect for a flashy *gin tonica*.

But it's not all about appearance. The wide opening serves up all the botanical scent your gin has to offer, and the stem keeps your dirty paws from warming up your drink.

Martini / cocktail

You know the kind. If I say to you, 'Picture James Bond drinking a cocktail,' this is the glass you imagine. A long dainty stem with a conical dish on top (or as I like to think of it – an upside-down triangle).

Martini glasses are designed for short drinks (such as a martini, obviously), and so don't hold much liquid. They're pleasing to the eye, they're delicate, and they're frustratingly easy to spill.

Coupe

Anything looks good in a coupe glass. Well, any short cocktail, that is.

A curved shallow bowl, often with straight-ish sides, on a stem. This is my wife's favourite glass shape – a frothy sour cocktail in a coupe will give her a sigh of bliss at the very first sip.

Nick & Nora

Named for the husband and wife detective team in the 1934 murder mystery *The Thin Man*, this glass shape is a deepish bowl on a stem – halfway between a champagne flute and a coupe glass. It's a small cocktail glass that's played a big role in the cocktail renaissance of the 2000s.

Cosmopolitan

I'm not sure why I get such strong Prohibition vibes from this conical glass on a small base . . . but I do. It's somehow fun and classy and naughty, all at the same time. Don't waste this glass on a cosmo – let it show off your aviation or gimlet.

Shot glass

Nope.

Glencairn

Glencairn glasses are for tasting spirits neat. Their tulip shape was originally designed for sipping whisky, but it works equally well for gin. It gives the liquid a wide surface area to release its aromatics, while the tapered mouth keeps those aromatics contained in the glass so they don't float away.

This glass makes you look like a professional taster (or a pretentious git, depending on your attitude).

And my personal favourite . . .

Rocks / old fashioned / lowball

If the highball tumbler is Bert, the lowball is Ernie.

Rocks, old fashioned, lowball, or even just whisky glass – these all refer to the same basic glass shape. This design is short and wide, usually cylindrical, often with a heavy base. With this glass, your nose is never far away from the aromatic oils in your gin.

I could live out my days with nothing but a rocks glass. (In fact, I own two kinds.) It's good for gin on the rocks, a strong G&T, a blazing red negroni or, hey, I'm even happy drinking a martini in a lowball. At least I'm not afraid I'll knock it over with the slightest bump.

The ice

You care about your gin. You care about your mixer. If you're going to make ice, you may as well love it as well.

The quality of the ice

Does it taste clean? If it's picked up a funny flavour – from the water out of your tap or the material the ice cube tray is made from, or even from other things in your freezer – it's worth finding a solution. Try filtering or boiling your water, buying a new ice cube tray, or storing your ice in a sealed container or ziplock bag.

Boss level: making perfectly clear ice. I gave up after a few attempts. It's truly a labour of love.

The size and shape of the ice

On the functional side, the larger the pieces of ice, the slower they will melt. Don't ask me about the science behind this: something something transfer of energy, surface area, first law of thermodynamics (probably). But large ice won't dilute your drink as quickly.

On the aesthetic side, your pieces of ice can come in different forms. I'm not a huge fan of novelty shapes (stars, lovehearts, sinking *Titanic* etc.), but I adore a huge cube that fills my rocks glass.

Boss level: freezing blocks of ice and breaking off chunks with special tools. Tell your loved ones in advance, so when they see you buying a tiny ice pick, they're not afraid you're about to commit an Agatha Christie–style murder.

Not all ice is just frozen water

If you make ice cubes out of tonic water, they won't make your G&T watery as they melt. The same goes for making ice with any other mixer.

You can step up your ice game by freezing your garnish into aesthetically pleasing ice cubes. Mint leaves frozen in ice cubes – or strawberries, or citrus wedges, or star anise – have a fantastic effort-to-impressiveness ratio.

Cold tips

It's tempting to use less ice if you don't want your drink to get watery. But it's actually the other way around: the more ice you put in there, the slower it will melt and dilute your drink. Fill the glass at least halfway with ice before adding the liquid.

Want your ice to last longer? Keep your gin and any other ingredients in the fridge, so they're already chilled when they go in your drink.

Crushed ice – the kind they give you in a bad pub – will melt faster than the Wicked Witch of the West. You've been warned.

The garnish

Gone are the days when a lemon wheel or lime wedge are your only options as a garnish for a G&T.

(Though for classic cocktails, I recommend sticking with their classic garnishes – a gimlet has a lime wheel, a negroni goes well with an orange wheel or twist, and a martini calls for olives, a lemon twist or pickled onions.)

Eat with your eyes . . . and your mouth

Garnishes are pleasing to the eye, and they ensure we start enjoying our drink even before it reaches our lips. And let's be honest, a well-decorated drink makes for good photos.

But unless you're garnishing your drink with a plastic dinosaur, you want something that makes your drink smell and/or taste even better. Choose a garnish that sits in harmony with the botanicals in the gin, or with flavours that complement and contrast. In other words, think either: 'Pair citrus with a citrussy drink' or 'What goes well with citrus?'

Eat with your eyes, not your mouth

If you're loading your drink up with curly straws and sparklers, I'm not sure there's anything I can do to help you.

But some garnishes do look better than they taste. Lavender and star anise look pretty, but I don't want them in my mouth.

My solution: freeze them into ice cubes. (Now that I think about it, this would also work for plastic dinosaurs.)

Fresh is best

Soggy berries. Wilting mint leaves. These are fine in a smoothie, but not as a decoration. Don't ruin an excellent drink with an unappealing garnish. Only use fresh fruit, herbs etc. that you'd happily eat and serve to guests.

Hot tip

Dehydrated garnishes play by different rules. They look good and they last a long time in a sealed container

You can buy packs of dried citrus wheels, apple slices, edible flowers, juniper berries etc. or you can dehydrate anything yourself. Keep some dried garnishes on hand at all times, and you'll never find yourself panicking because there's no fresh garnish available.

Get creative

Between fruits, vegetables, herbs, spices, leaves and flowers . . . you won't run out of garnish options any time soon.

For each drink, keep to one or two garnishes for best effect. ('It's a drink, not a salad!')

Here are a few ideas to get you started:

- **Rosemary skewered through blueberries.** If you grow the rosemary yourself, you can even include some of the purple flowers.

- **Strawberry and basil** make a summery and surprising combo.

- **The zing of lemon and a crunch of pepper** will keep you on your toes. Pair with a powerful, juniper-heavy G&T.

- **The freshness of cucumber is unmatched.** Pair it with raspberries for a tart lift, chamomile flowers for a softer touch, or sweet rose petals to see why Hendrick's fell in love.

- **Flamed cinnamon quill and a slice of orange tastes** like warmth in winter. Just the thing for a mulled sloe gin or a spiced gin with soda water.

- **Dried pineapple and mint** are about as tropical as it gets. (People talk about slapping mint to wake it up. What an obnoxious way to be woken. What did the mint ever do to you?)

- **Take a risk with some bolder flavours:** a curl of ginger and a stalk of lemongrass, some mandarin peel and a strip of chilli, or a sprig of thyme with sweet cherry tomatoes. There are no limits.

137

Let's do the twist

When citrus twists were first introduced to cocktails in the 1800s, it was to prove to the drinker that fresh juice had been used to make the drink (as opposed to cordial). Nowadays, we use them because they're attractive to the eye and pleasing to the nose.

Making the ideal citrus twist takes some practice. But it's a simple skill worth developing,.

1. Using a sharp knife or a vegetable peeler, remove a strip of citrus peel about as long and as wide as your pinky finger.

2. Lay it on the bench with the pith (the white stuff on the inside) facing up. Use a knife to shave off as much of the pith as you reasonably can.

3. It's up to you whether you keep the shape of the twist *au naturel* or tidy it up with a knife.

4. Either twist or curl the peel, but do it above your glass – the essential oils will mist into the air, and you want them to land on your drink.

5. Hang the peel over the edge of the glass or drop it into the drink.

Variations

Cut the twist as above, roll it up, then pierce through all the layers with a toothpick.

Cut the peel from a citrus wheel, remove the pith, and wind the peel around a straw or chopstick to make a tight spring.

A coin-sized circle of peel is simple but striking.

Ways to drink gin

Distillers put so much time and effort and passion and expertise into creating a layered, nuanced spirit. But that part of the process comes to an end when the gin goes into the bottle.

From there, the next stage begins: how do we get the stuff into our gullets?

Or if you want to avoid the inexplicably gross word 'gullet', you might ask: what's the best way to appreciate gin in all its glory?

There is no one answer, and it's not as straightforward as with some other drinks. When you want to drink wine, you simply pour a glass of it. But with gin, there are more options . . .

Gin and tonic

Some dynamic duos are so intertwined, it's hard to say one without the other. Bonnie and Clyde. Timon and Pumbaa. Romeo and Juliet. Gin and tonic.

The G&T is the most popular way gin is consumed around the world. In fact, for many people who say they don't like gin, it's actually bitter tonic water they don't like . . . but they've only ever tasted them together.

Gin and tonic has its origin in the 1800s – British colonisers in India were taking a daily dose of quinine to protect them from malaria, which led to the development of 'tonic water' – a sweeter way to take the medicine. But even this Mary Poppins–approved product could be made more pleasant with a generous dose of gin. The gin and tonic was born, and quickly made its way back to Europe.

As an anti-malaria medicine, the drink did its job. The ever quotable Winston Churchill said, 'The gin and tonic has saved more Englishmen's lives, and minds, than all the doctors in the Empire.'

As something to drink for pleasure, gin and tonics are now a beloved icon of English culture: tea and toast in the morning, gin and tonic in the afternoon.

A brief history of tonic water

Tonic water (or 'Indian tonic water') is a carbonated soft drink made with quinine, sweetener and citrus.

Its bitter taste comes from quinine, from the bark of the cinchona tree. From the time Europeans saw Peruvian tribes using it medicinally in the 1600s, cinchona bark became a valuable commodity. For hundreds of years it was the centre of a trade monopoly, and was seen as the secret weapon in global wars – whoever owned the quinine owned the tropics.

The first commercial tonic water hit the market in 1858, and Schweppes released their version 12 years later. Over the years, tonic water evolved from a medicinal product medicine to a cheap mixer full of artificial flavourings and sweeteners. But the rise of artisanal spirits has spurred the rise of premium mixers, including tonic waters.

You can find a flavoured tonic water to complement the botanicals of any great gin – some are more citrussy, floral, fruity or herbal. Or use classic tonic water and enjoy a classic drink.

G&T – a simple drink with endless options

There are two schools of thought when it comes to gin and tonic.

The first school of thought: 'You can't stuff up a gin and tonic.'

The gin and tonic is idiot-proof, and this is what makes it so wonderful. Walk into a bar with stale beer on the floor and bad country music in the air, and you can still get a G&T that tastes like a G&T. And anybody can make one at home without cocktail equipment or skills.

It's easy. It's safe. It's familiar.

But some people come from a different direction. They say, 'I respect gin too much to let someone ruin it with cheap tonic water – or, horror of horrors, *flat* tonic water. I don't want it diluted with crushed ice or tainted with a flaccid slice of lemon.'

Which brings us to the second school of thought: 'What's better than a good gin and tonic? A *great* gin and tonic.'

The gin

Gin and tonics usually use a London dry or new world gin, but Plymouth or navy strength work well too.

Some gin snobs argue that expensive or subtle gins should never be sullied with tonic water, but I reckon if you've got your hands on a gin that you can't wait to taste, have a go. It's all about making your ideal G&T, not meeting someone else's standards.

The tonic water

You can find Schweppes tonic water almost anywhere in the world. It's been around for over 150 years, and it does the job just fine. But there's better tonic to be had.

You can't go wrong with Fever-Tree and its range of premium tonic waters.

If you're ready to dive deep, visit specialty bottle shops to discover local or artisanal tonics. Some people even buy tonic water syrup and mix it with soda water to their preferred strength or make their own tonic water. (Impressive, but too much effort for me!)

Hot tip

Buy tonic water in small bottles or cans. Yes, they're more expensive by volume than the large bottles, but it's a small price to pay. Unless you're sharing a big bottle, you'll put it in the fridge half-full, and it'll lose fizz and make your next G&T second-rate.

With the small bottles, every single G&T you drink is lively as it should be.

The glass

A highball glass or a rocks tumbler is a fine choice for a G&T. If you want to get serious, you might get yourself a copa de balon – Spanish balloon glass – to maximise the aroma of the gin and show off the beautiful garnishes.

Personally, I want my gin and tonic in one of two glasses: a dainty stemless wine glass that shows everyone how classy I am, or a chunky heavy crystal whisky tumbler that I could use as a weapon in a bar fight. Not interested in anything in between.

The method

It's simple, and you don't need to overcomplicate it.

Fill the glass with ice – at least half the glass.

Pour in the gin next – this gets it nice and cold.

Next, add your (always cold) tonic water. A mixologist may pour the tonic down a spoon so as not to disturb the carbonation, but that's too fiddly for me. I pour it in gently, and it's never caused a shortage of effervescence.

You may like to end with a gentle stir to make sure the drink is mixed and as cold as possible.

A glowing review

Tonic water glows under ultraviolet light (it's the quinine). If you shine a black light over it – or order a G&T at a hip club where black lights are the norm – you'll find yourself drinking something that looks radioactive.

The ratio

How much gin, and how much tonic?

The most common ratios are between 1:1 and 1:4.

I like my flavours punchy, so equal measures gin and tonic suits me wonderfully – a short, strong drink that expresses the character of the gin with the tonic just taking the edge off.

If you prefer a long drink to sip on a hot summer's afternoon, you may be more of a 1:4 person. Weaker than this and you're starting to miss a lot of the gin's flavours.

You don't have to measure the amounts; you can always just eyeball it. But once you know how you like it, you may find that measuring is the only surefire way to hit your perfect strength.

The garnish

You can play it safe with a slice of citrus, but safety is overrated.

Look to the gin's botanicals and choose a fruit or herb that magnifies those flavours. Don't be afraid to look beyond the usual suspects. (See 'Serving up your gin: the garnish' on page 135 for ideas.)

Live dangerously and see what works.

Want ideas for where to start?

A drier, more classic London dry? Experiment with fun and interesting tonics. Find something local and artisanal – maybe even do a side-by-side tasting.

A citrussy gin? Decide whether you want to double down with a citrussy tonic, or whether you want to contrast it with, say, a Mediterranean-style herbal tonic.

A new world gin with a very distinct botanical flavour? Don't overpower it – use a plainer tonic.

A gin with subtle botanical flavours? Choose a less potent tonic, but also just use less tonic – a 1:1 ratio will ensure those nuances don't get lost.

There's a wrong way to make a G&T (please don't use flat tonic and funky lime), but there's no right way. Get creative. Experiment. Try different garnishes. Discover what you like . . . then keep exploring.

You'll find some great combinations, and your friends will find you interesting.

Other mixers

Don't like the bitterness or taste of tonic water, or simply want other options for a long, refreshing gin drink? No problem – let's explore.

Most of my thoughts in the gin and tonic section – about selecting the gin, the glass, the ratio etc. – apply here, too. And as with tonic, don't go cheap on the mixer. It's worth forking out a few extra bucks for the good stuff.

This kind of drink is all about supporting and lengthening the gin, not trying to block it out. Don't overdo it, or you'll lose the taste of gin. It's better to pour too little mixer than too much – you can always add more.

Soda water or club soda is such a pure way to enjoy gin. Gin and soda says 'yes' to bubbles but 'no' to added bitterness or sweetness, bringing the refreshment of a long drink without introducing any new flavours (or calories, if that matters to you). The carbonation releases aroma into the air like the olfactory version of throwing confetti.

Citrus soft drinks with gin just make sense. San Pellegrino and Fever-Tree are two widely available premium brands, but if you look around you're bound to find others. As a general guide: lemon will focus on sourness and boost the citrus in your gin; orange will focus on sweetness, so will lay the groundwork for other botanicals like spices to shine; grapefruit will bring a new dimension of bitterness. The best way to find your favourite is to try them all yourself. Have a mixer tasting in the morning, then a gin tasting in the afternoon!

Gin and juice is a popular way to go – Snoop Dogg and Lou Bega both sing about it. Orange juice is the most common option. Grapefruit juice is tart, tangy and bitter – and if you salt the rim, you've made yourself a salty dog cocktail. Cranberry juice provides a tart sweetness and slightly grippy texture to your gin – and its gorgeous colour, of course. Apple juice with a spiced gin can give a mulled cider vibe.

Ginger ale and ginger beer both add sweet and warming spice to your drink, so you'll want to be choosy about what gin you pick – go for something robust enough to hold its own, like a gin that contains ginger or has a notable cinnamon kick. Ginger ale is lighter and sweeter, while ginger beer is heavier and spicier. Plus, 'gin and ginger' is fun to say. Just rolls off the tongue, doesn't it?

Cola may seem like an odd choice to mix with gin, but in Spain it's all the rage. Go with a mid-range gin with an aggressive flavour – a junipery punch, a spicy bite, a citrussy headbutt. Use an artisanal cola if possible and keep the ratio of gin to cola high (try 1:2 or 2:3). Colas are flavoured with ingredients like vanilla, citrus, cinnamon and kola nut, so call it a dark botanical soda and your friends will think you've found something exotic.

Chinotto is an Italian cola flavoured with a bitter Italian orange of the same name. It's the same fruit that gives Campari its bitterness.

Homemade iced tea is making a comeback. I say homemade because the bottled stuff is always sweetened out the wazoo. But brew up some English Breakfast or Earl Grey, perhaps add a little lemon or peach, and make a pitcher of iced tea and gin for when the neighbours mosey on over.

No mixer

I've heard people talk like you shouldn't drink gin neat – like you're strange if you do, or you're ignorant, or you're just plain drinking it wrong.

But drinking any spirit in its natural state, without other flavours added, is a great way to get to know its true character. Gin has a bounty of treasures to offer: the aromas, the textures, the layers of botanicals, the finish . . . there's gold in them thar hills! And with the plethora of botanicals that make their way into gin, it makes sense to approach them face to face to see what they're like. A nice gin will offer up plenty of nuance. A cheaper gin will convince you that it's designed to be mixed.

Any time I crack open a new bottle of gin, the first thing I do is taste it by itself. It's a great way to get a sense of it before mixing it with anything. If you truly want to taste the distinctives between gin styles, between different distilleries and brands and between individual gins . . . this is the no-brainer way to do it.

Of course, there's a good chance that after trying a gin neat, you'll want it a different way, and that's perfectly fine. That doesn't mean the experiment was a failure. It means it was a success – you now have a better sense of the gin and how you want to drink it.

Is there a reason not to drink gin without a mixer?

No. No good reason, at least.

Over the centuries, gin has developed a culture of mixing, from using gin to disguise the bitterness of tonic water to using sugar and fruits to disguise the flaws in poor quality gin. People settled comfortably into drinking gin with mixers and in cocktails, and never really went back to drinking it on its own.

Nowadays, the most common reason I hear is: 'The taste is too harsh.' Which usually means they've only ever tasted bad gin, which isn't pleasant to drink neat. Either that, or the person simply doesn't like the taste of juniper (yet). Just like beer and whisky and red wine, gin is an acquired taste.

Here's a few ways to go about it . . .

Neat (on its own)

This is just the spirit poured into a glass, usually a rocks glass. Sometimes called 'straight'.

With neat gin, the spirit is naked and exposed with nothing to hide behind. Drinking gin neat can be confronting if you've never done it before, and for good reason – it's intense (gintense?). But think of it like a big cat handler inviting you to pat a tiger. You'll want to be careful, and approach it with a sense of gravity . . . but it'll likely be a thrilling experience, and you'll be glad you took hold of the opportunity.

This is not 'doing a shot' of gin. Doing shots is about tasting the drink as little as possible – the opposite of what we're trying to do. Neat is for sipping. The warmth, the bare botanicals, the transition from smell to sip to aftertaste . . . savour it.

On the rocks (with ice)

This is the spirit in a glass with ice cubes, usually in a rocks glass – this is where the glass gets its name!

Ice cools the spirit down, which can smooth off the sharper corners of the gin's flavour. And as the ice melts and slightly dilutes the gin, the alcohol burn starts to back off so you can taste the botanicals more clearly.

This is an evolving drink – it'll continue to cool and dilute as the ice slowly melts. Appreciate the difference.

Give your glass a swirl to start the cooling and diluting process and enjoy the glorious clinking sound of the ice against the glass or crystal. There's nothing like it.

Up (chilled with ice then strained)

This is the spirit stirred or shaken with ice to chill and slightly dilute the spirit, but then strained so there's no ice served in your glass. It's usually served in a cocktail glass. Sometimes called 'straight up', though that's more for cocktails.

While gin on the rocks will keep changing as it dilutes, gin served up is a finished product.

With water

It's so simple, but adding water helps the botanicals in a gin to reveal their nuances.

Imagine you have a piece of intricately patterned fabric scrunched up in a ball. Now imagine unfurling it so you can enjoy its full beauty and notice all the details you couldn't see before. That's what adding water does to gin – opens it up. Delicate botanicals that were hidden behind alcohol heat can step out into the light.

A little water wakes up the flavours of the gin. Too much puts them back to sleep. Find the ratio that works best for you. Some people mix gin 1:1 with water. Some just add a few drops, which opens up the flavour while keeping the oomph of the booze.

This way, the gin is still mostly naked; it's just wearing a hat.

Cocktails

If you go to bartending school, you can learn about all the different categories of cocktails. But I like to keep it simple, so I break cocktails into two kinds: short and long.

Short cocktails are intense. They're generally under 100 ml (3⅓ fl oz) and contain an equal or higher proportion of alcoholic ingredients to non-alcoholic ingredients; there's little or no mixer. A short drink is full-on in flavour, and can hit you like a bus if you're not ready for it. But if you are ready for it, you can sit back and let it take you where you want to go. Also like a bus, I suppose.

Long cocktails are more easy-going and refreshing. They contain more non-alcoholic ingredients (soda water, juice etc.), and often sit around the 200–250 ml (6⅔–8⅓ fl oz) mark. A long cocktail may contain the same alcohol as a short cocktail, but since it's lengthened and diluted it doesn't have the same intense punch.

Most cocktails fit cleanly into one of these two categories.

- **A martini**, which is just gin and vermouth? Short.

- **An aviation**, which brings together gin with maraschino liqueur, creme de violet and lemon juice? Short.

- **A Tom Collins**, which lengthens gin, lemon juice and simple syrup with soda water? Long.

- **A Singapore sling**, where the gin and cherry brandy and Bénédictine join forces with fruit juices and soda water to make a drink best poured from a jug? Long.

Both long and short cocktails have their place. It depends what kind of experience you're after. Do you want the gin to shine with help from another ingredient, or do you want it to be part of a complex blend? Do you want a drink that transforms the gin into something sharp and sour or spicy and syrupy, or do you want it to refresh you on a warm evening?

Cocktails are all about making new taste combinations. Tradition is great – the International Bartenders Association (IBA) Official Cocktail List has you sorted there. But experimentation and evolution are great, too. With new spirits, new ingredients, new bartenders and new technologies . . . it would be absolutely insane if these didn't lead to new cocktail recipes.

Making cocktails

I quite like a short cocktail that's a lot of gin and a little of something else – a dry martini, an old fashioned, a pink gin. These simple cocktails are designed to maintain the subtleties of the gin.

Others might lean more towards the bracing bite of a sour. Others still something tall, fresh and fruity.

And of course, many gin lovers will rightly say: 'Depends on the occasion, depends on my mood, depends on the gin!'

Considering the most common reason we drink is to have fun, it can be confronting to see how many 'rules' there are in the world of cocktails. Making cocktails is an expertise all in itself, and there are people who have spent decades mastering the art. I have a lot of respect for them . . . but I'm not one of them.

There are plenty of helpful resources out there just waiting to teach you the Proper Rules for making Proper Cocktails.

Me? I'm just here to have fun.

What equipment do I need?

Most kitchens have a measuring cup/jug, a bottle opener, a sharp knife and a vegetable peeler. We've already discussed glassware, ice and garnishes (see 'Serving up your gin' on page 129). I wouldn't bother with one of those cocktail kits with a long bar spoon and a muddling stick and what have you.

To get started, these are the only 'special' items you need:

- A 30 ml or 50 ml (1 fl oz or 1⅔ fl oz) measuring glass designed for spirits or espresso.

- A cocktail shaker. I suggest a stainless steel one rather than a cheap plastic one – it won't collect colour or smells, and it looks classy.

- Toothpicks.

A few key ingredients . . .

Simple syrup

This is a common cocktail ingredient, especially in recipes containing citrus juice. It's just a sweetener made of sugar and water, and it's easy to make.

- 1 cup (8 oz) regular white sugar
- 1 cup (8⅓ fl oz) hot water (from tap or kettle)

Combine the sugar and water.

Stir until dissolved.

Simple, right? Or to make rich sugar syrup . . .

- 2 cups (16 oz) regular white sugar
- 1 cup (8⅓ fl oz) water

Put them in a pot on the stove

Bring them to the boil (briefly) to get the sugar to dissolve properly.

Why not just use sugar in my drink? It's hard to dissolve in alcohol and cold drinks, so it'll leave grains of sugar at the bottom of your glass.

Can I add one cup (8 oz) of sugar to a measuring jug then add water up to the two cup (16⅔ fl oz) mark? No – because of the air between grains of sugar, this method uses much more water and throws the ratio off. Measure each ingredient separately.

Do I have to use regular white sugar? It's ideal – it dissolves quickly, it's almost clear in colour, and it gives a clean sweetness with neutral flavour. Other kinds of sugar change the colour and flavour of your cocktails.

How do I store it? In a clean glass container in the fridge; a glass bottle with a lid is easiest to use. Try a maple syrup bottle, or even an old gin bottle.

How long will it last? At least a month in the fridge. Longer if you make it with boiling water or boil it on the stove.

Juice

Lemon or lime juice should be freshly squeezed. Lemons and limes last quite well in the fridge, so they're easy to keep on hand most of the time.

(Note: cut your citrus wheel garnish and/or peel your lemon twists before cutting and juicing the fruit.)

For other juices, if you're not juicing the fruit yourself, buy the best quality juice available. It's worth a couple of extra bucks to make a magnificent cocktail rather than a mediocre one.

Aquafaba

Literally means 'bean water', but don't let that put you off.

It's the liquid strained from a can of chickpeas or other low-flavour legumes, and it's an impressive alternative to egg. In cocktails (and cooking), 30 ml (1 fl oz) aquafaba replaces one egg white or 45 ml (1½ fl oz) replaces a whole egg.

Many bartenders prefer it to egg and use aquafaba as standard for frothing drinks – it has a lovely texture, and a more neutral smell and taste than egg whites. (Once it's in the drink, that is. Ignore the weird smell when you open the can – it doesn't carry across.)

Choose a brand of chickpeas with no added salt (or the least amount of salt). Store a few cans in the cupboard and you'll never have to separate egg whites again.

Martini (dry)

Gin and dry vermouth. It sounds so basic when you say it like that. But the martini has been immortalised in our collective consciousness as an icon of pizazz and panache. How can one drink conjure up images of Hollywood starlets and prime ministers, sequinned cocktail dresses and tailored tuxedos?

Back in the day, it was common to have a 2:1 ratio of gin to vermouth, but over the years the martini has been getting drier (less vermouth) –probably because gin has been getting better. The IBA recipe calls for a 6:1 ratio, so let's use that as our starting point.

- 60 ml (2 fl oz) gin
- 10 ml (⅓ fl oz) dry (white) verm outh

    Pour the gin and vermouth into a cold mixing glass or shaker, full of ice.

    Stir, stir, stir – for at least 45 seconds. You want your martini to be so cold you get goosebumps.

    Strain the drink into a chilled martini glass.

Garnish with one of the following . . .

- **Olives.** Bright green Sicilian olives are my pick – one or three on a toothpick. The martini-soaked olives at the end of your drink are some of the best things a human can eat.

- **A lemon twist.** It's incredibly aesthetic, and its spritz of oils expressed over the surface of your drink adds a zingy element.

- **Pickled (cocktail) onions.** Again, one or three on a toothpick. They give your drink a savoury bite, and turn it into a gibson martini.

- **I'll also accept a cornichon or three.** Mostly because I like the word 'cornichon'.

A few notes:

Most bartenders will stir martinis as standard since shaking can 'bruise the gin' (lose some of the volatile aromatics or top notes of the gin), change the texture of your drink and increase the dilution. But if you prefer your martini shaken, own it with confidence. Your drink order is your drink order.

There's a legend that Winston Churchill's martini preference was ice cold Plymouth gin and 'a bow in the direction of France' (the home of dry vermouth). But a gin martini is best when you include both ingredients.

The martini is a very personal cocktail. Everyone has their own idea about how to make one, so tweak the recipe to your heart's content. Try different ratios, different glasses – and, of course, different gins – to discover your preference. The only rule? You then have to swear to people that your way is the best way.

How would you like it?

50/50 or halfsies – equal measures gin and vermouth

Wet – three parts gin to one part vermouth

Dry – six parts gin to one part vermouth

Extra dry – at least a 10:1 ratio, or maybe just a splash of vermouth

Bone dry – coat the inside of the glass with vermouth then tip it out, or no vermouth at all (just gin served up)

Perfect – the vermouth is split 50% dry vermouth, 50% sweet (red) vermouth

Dirty – some brine from the olives is added to your martini (ask for it filthy if you want even more brine)

Gibson – a dry martini garnished with a pickled onion or three

A French martini is not a martini. An espresso martini is not a martini. An appletini is not a martini. These might be fine drinks . . . but they're not martinis.

Negroni

1919: Italian nobleman Count Camillo Negroni walks into Caffè Casoni in Florence and orders an Americano cocktail, but tells the bartender to make it stronger by subbing out the soda water for gin. The bartender complies, and swaps the lemon slice for an orange slice. The negroni is born.

2020: In the middle of a pandemic lockdown, Italian-American actor Stanley Tucci shares a video of himself making a negroni in his kitchen at home.

He uses different proportions to the IBA standard, and instead of stirring, he shakes and serves it up. The video goes viral. The negroni is still popular.

(For the record, I think shaking a negroni is madness. But the Tooch has done well for himself, so perhaps I should be more open-minded.)

Italians gave this drink to the world, and I couldn't be more grateful. Because just like Italians, negronis are intense and full of life. It's why we love them.

- 30 ml (1 fl oz) gin (a strong London dry works best)
- 30 ml (1 fl oz) Campari
- 30 ml (1 fl oz) sweet (red) vermouth

Pour all ingredients over plenty of ice in a chilled rocks glass. Stir gently to mix. Alternatively, stir with ice in a shaker, then strain into your glass of choice.

Garnish with an orange twist or a whole orange wheel.

Stirred, not shaken

A stirred negroni is silky smooth and bitingly bitter and syrupy sweet. It's meant to be.

But if you want it extra cold and more diluted, you can shake it. In my house, this has come to be known as a Tucci. There's no putting that genie back in the bottle.

Old fashioned gin cocktail

Once upon a time, a 'cocktail' was a specific style of drink: any spirit with added sugar, water and bitters.

Fast forward to the early 20th century when mixed drinks were wildly popular, and 'cocktails' were now full of fruity and fancy ingredients. A traditionalist could instead ask the bartender to just mix a drink 'the old fashioned way'.

Nowadays, an 'old fashioned' is usually made on whisk(e)y, but Harry Craddock's *The Savoy Cocktail Book* published in 1930 lists gin as one of the spirits you can use to make an old fashioned cocktail. Or go back further to Jerry Thomas's 1862 book *The Bar-Tenders Guide* where you'll find a recipe for an old fashioned with 'Holland gin' – genever.

Now that's old fashioned.

- 60 ml (2 fl oz) gin (a barrel-aged gin brings lovely complexity)
- 5 ml (1 tsp) rich sugar syrup
- A few dashes Angostura bitters

Stir ingredients in a mixing glass with ice, then strain into an old fashioned (rocks) glass with one large fresh ice cube if possible (otherwise other ice).

Garnish with an orange twist.

If you want to be really old fashioned, you can use a sugar cube instead of sugar syrup. Good luck dissolving it.

Gimlet

Want to make a 'proper' gimlet? Equal parts gin and Rose's Lime Juice Cordial. But, uh . . . it's not very nice. Who'd have thought sailors in the 1800s couldn't make delicious cocktails on long-haul sea voyages?

Actually, the main reason is because Rose's is mostly artificial nowadays. So: want to make the best gimlet? Make your own lime syrup (closer to how Rose's used to be) ahead of time.

Want to make a quick gimlet with no lime syrup? You can cheat.

Best gimlet

- 50 ml (1⅔ fl oz) gin
- 50 ml (1⅔ fl oz) lime syrup

  Shake with ice for 20 seconds, then strain into a chilled coupe glass.

  Garnish with a lime wheel.

Cheat's gimlet

- 50 ml (1⅔ fl oz) gin
- 25 ml (¾ fl oz) lime juice
- 25 ml (¾ fl oz) simple syrup
- The lime shells from the lime(s) you juiced

  Add everything including the peel to a cocktail shaker and shake with ice for 20 seconds, then strain into a chilled coupe glass. (Discard the peel.)

  Garnish with a lime wheel.

The version with lime syrup is sweeter, and the lime flavour is more integrated. The cheat version is less sweet, more tart and has a bitter lime peel kick. But it'll do in a pinch, and you may even prefer it that way.

And you don't have to be precious about a gimlet, anyway. Higher ratio of gin? More lime juice? Whatever. It'll still protect you from scurvy.

Lime syrup

1 cup (8⅓ fl oz) water

1 cup (8 oz) sugar

Zest of 2 limes

Juice of (the same) 2 limes

Put the water, sugar and lime zest into a small saucepan. Heat gently, stirring constantly, until the sugar is dissolved. Refrigerate for at least a couple of hours; once it's cool, stir in the lime juice.

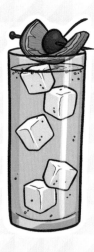

Tom Collins

The Great Tom Collins Hoax of 1874 was a trend in New York and Pennsylvania. It was a practical joke you'd play on your friend, and went something like this:

You: 'Have you seen Tom Collins?'

Friend: 'Why, I don't believe I know a Tom Collins.'

You: 'He says he knows you. He's in a bar around the corner, claiming you collect ladies' undergarments and that your moustache is false.'

Friend: 'I say, what a cad! I'll give him what for. In the bar around the corner, you say?' *rushes off to find Tom Collins while rolling up sleeves to prepare for fisticuffs*

That's the joke. I guess people were easily amused in ye olde days.

Anyway, shortly after this, the Tom Collins cocktail started showing up in American cocktail books in homage to the hoax. Or maybe the whole thing was just a guerilla marketing campaign by Big Collins.

- 50 ml (1⅔ fl oz) Old Tom gin
- 25 ml (¾ fl oz) lemon juice
- 15 ml (½ fl oz) simple syrup
- Soda water

Shake the gin, lemon juice and simple syrup in a cocktail shaker with ice, then strain into a Collins glass with fresh ice cubes. Top up with soda water and stir gently.

Garnish with an orange or lemon wheel folded around a maraschino cherry and skewered through with a toothpick. Fiddly, but it looks nice.

If you use London dry instead of Old Tom, use rich sugar syrup to hold on to the lemonade-y sweetness.

Gin sour

Sours are an old family of cocktails – you'll find a recipe for a gin sour in *The Bar-Tenders Guide* from 1862. They've made their home on modern cocktail menus because they do a superb job of balancing their three flavours – sweet and sour and strong.

- 60 ml (2 fl oz) gin
- 30 ml (1 fl oz) lemon juice
- 15 ml (½ fl oz) sugar syrup
- 15 ml (½ fl oz) aquafaba or half an egg white
- A few dashes of Angostura bitters

Add the ingredients to a shaker. Dry shake (shake without ice) to froth the drink, then add ice and shake until cold. Strain into a chilled glass.

Stain the foam with a few dashes of Angostura bitters. You can also garnish by carefully floating a dehydrated citrus wheel on top of the foam. (Learn from my mistake – fresh citrus collapses the foam.)

You can technically leave out the aquafaba/egg white (and skip the dry shaking step), but I reckon the froth is non-negotiable – it ties the flavours together like nothing else, gives the drink a smooth texture and looks beautiful resting atop the liquid.

Paddington's negroni sour

There are other variations on the negroni, but this is the best one. My wife and I discovered it during the pandemic, when we had a weekly cocktail club with friends over Zoom.

The negroni sweetness cuts through the sourness; the frothy smoothness rounds off the edge of the negroni's bitterness; the sour lengthens the negroni, making it slightly less intense but more refreshing; the use of marmalade instead of simple syrup makes the sour more vibrant.

Just superb balance all round.

Credit for this cocktail goes to chef Mike Denman, and to Dunnet Bay Distillers with their Rock Rose Gin. I've bastardised the recipe slightly; this is how I make it at home.

- 30 ml (1 fl oz) gin

- 30 ml (1 fl oz) sweet (red) vermouth

- 30 ml (1 fl oz) Campari

- 30 ml (1 fl oz) lemon juice (or slightly less)

- 30 ml (1 fl oz) aquafaba

- 1 tbsp (⅔ fl oz) orange marmalade

- A few dashes of Angostura bitters

Add the ingredients to a shaker. Dry shake (shake without ice) to froth the drink, then add ice and shake until cold.

Strain into a chilled coupe or rocks glass.

Stain the foam with a few dashes of Angostura bitters.

Garnish with an orange twist, or by carefully floating a dehydrated orange wheel on top of the foam.

Gin-gin mule

The 'mule' is a reference to the Moscow mule cocktail.

The second 'gin' is for ginger.

The first 'gin' is for . . . gin.

Sipping a gin-gin mule gives you that 'life is good' feeling. The mint and lime are a huge lift to the ginger flavour, and the gin brings more to the party than vodka ever did.

The gin-gin mule was invented in 2000 by bartender Audrey Saunders, a key figure in the craft cocktail movement in New York.

- Mint leaves (about 8 should do it)
- 30 ml (1 fl oz) simple syrup
- 50 ml (1⅔ fl oz) gin
- 25 ml (¾ fl oz) lime juice
- Ginger beer

Muddle the mint leaves and sugar syrup in the bottom of a cocktail shaker; bruise the leaves, but don't break them up.

Add the gin and lime juice and a handful of ice and shake well.

Strain into a highball or Collins glass with fresh ice cubes and top up with ginger beer.

Garnish with a sprig of mint and a wedge of lime.

No need to use an expensive or nuanced gin for this; use a middle-range gin with a kick. (Like a mule – get it?)

Some recipes suggest slapping the mint before adding it to the shaker. I tried that once and the mint flew across the room. I haven't done it since.

Mulled sloe gin

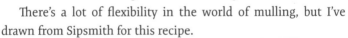

Hit sloe gin with a wash of spices and you've landed on the taste of Christmas.

I've given proportions rather than specific measurements, because while you could make a single cup of this, it's much better done as a larger batch for sharing.

There's a lot of flexibility in the world of mulling, but I've drawn from Sipsmith for this recipe.

- 2 parts hot water

- 2 parts cloudy apple juice

- Whole spices, e.g. cinnamon stick, star anise, cloves, cardamom pods, vanilla pod (cut down the middle) . . .

- 1 part sloe gin

  Warm everything except the sloe gin in a pan until just below boiling and simmer for 5–10 minutes. Take off the heat – and maybe put some aside as a non-alc option – and add the sloe gin.

Ladle into mugs; best to strain it if you don't want cloves in your teeth or star anise stuck in your throat.

Garnish each cup with half an orange slice and/or a stick of cinnamon.

Here are a few more classics you can look into for yourself . . .

Aviation: a variation on a gin sour that uses crème de violette to bring a floral touch and a gorgeous purple hue. Yes, Aviation Gin's floral notes sit excellently in this cocktail.

Corpse reviver #2: a 'morning after' cocktail that's supposedly a hangover cure; according to *The Savoy Cocktail Book* of 1930, 'Four of these taken in swift succession will revive the corpse again.' Yikes.

French 75: a gin-based champagne cocktail made with lemon juice and sugar. It's named after a French 75 mm field gun that was used in the First World War.

Martinez: widely held to be the precursor to a dry martini – though don't expect it to taste like one.

Pink gin: a simple mix of gin and Angostura bitters. Not to be confused with those berry-flavoured gins labelled 'pink gin'.

Ramos gin fizz: sweet and sour and creamy smooth and impossibly fluffy, it requires nine ingredients and 12 minutes to shake it properly. At the bar where it was created, they hired a bunch of shaker boys to shake this drink in relay!

Vesper: a variation on a martini invented by James Bond in Ian Fleming's 1953 novel *Casino Royale*. It contains an aperitif called Kina Lillet, which no longer exists, so Bond fans have been doing their best to recreate 007's signature drink ever since.

White lady: made with gin, triple sec and lemon juice. Famous bartender Harry Craddock had a habit of burying freshly mixed white ladies in walls in the 1920s and '30s as time capsules to be discovered in later decades.

Of course, this is just the tip of the huge, clear ice cube. Old and new, there are more gin drinks than you'll ever get around to in your life. But if you start now, you'll get at least a few good years in . . .

Making memories with gin

I once heard someone say, 'When you think of something you want to do, do it once, or do it every day.'

'Do it once' means make a big deal out of it. Look forward to it. Tell your friends about it, and maybe invite them into it. Take a few pictures and show them to people you love. Make it a Moment to Remember (capital M, capital R). When I found a pizza place near my house that sold pizza by the metre, I knew I wanted to eat a whole metre on my own – and I had friends who literally applauded me when I stuffed that final bite into my mouth. When I visited the Amalfi Coast with my wife, father-in-law and brother-in-law, I knew I wanted to drink a negroni at a clifftop bar while looking over the ocean – and we still bring up that shared experience any time we have a negroni together.

'Do it every day' may not literally mean every day, but it means incorporate this good thing into the rhythm of your life in a regular and repeated way. I have hot chips every single time I go to the beach. We have fresh mango and black coffee for breakfast every Christmas morning. For a long time, I met with a group of friends every month to taste gins and try a new cocktail. These things have worn memories deep into my mind in a different way – a slow drip, drip, drip that makes its mark over time.

Below are some of my favourite ideas of how gin can help you make memories and create lovely associations between a certain drink and a certain time, place, mood, activity or person. These ideas may capture your heart, or they may spark other ideas for you.

The only question is: do you want to do them once, or every day?

Sunny summer's day

I want to be outdoors, surrounded by green grass, dressed in navy shorts and a white linen shirt with the sleeves rolled up. I want a tall Tom Collins in my hand. And I kind of want to be playing bocce.

Sunset

Work is done for the day, or you're relaxed after a day of resting. The speakers are pumping with tunes to help you let go of any worries and get you in a good mood (I find Cat Empire is perfect for this). You've taken your shoes off.

This is prime G&T time.

Fill your glass with ice and pour a low-effort gin and tonic. That first one will be finished within a few minutes.

Take a little more time building your second drink. The alcohol from the first has just entered your veins, and you've begun to unwind. Your head feels 10% lighter – in a good way – and your limbs feel 10% heavier – also in a good way. So now you have the patience to mix your drink with the ideal measurements, to make sure the garnish is just right (or garnishes – glam it up, Spanish *gin tonica* style!), and to pay attention to the flavours of that first sip. Eat some chips, or pickles, or whatever go-to salty snack you like as you forget everything that's come before; ignore everything ahead of you, and just float in the here and now.

The sunlight is dying, but you couldn't feel more alive.

Cold winter night

The air outside is crisp, but I'm inside. The doors and windows are all closed. My friends are around (slightly too many for the space). The mugs are brimming with mulled sloe gin. I'm eating apple pie. Life is good.

Dinner party – Italian

Serving a round of negronis before dinner is the power move of the ultimate host. The bear hug of bitterness and syrupy kiss are the warmest welcome anyone could want

Follow this up with big bowls of pasta, passionate conversation and raucous laughter – and maybe another negroni – and you'll make memories that'll last for years to come.

Now that's my kind of hospitality.

Christmas

So many options!

If you see a Christmas gin at the bottle shop – maybe made with Christmas pudding, or cranberries, or gingerbread spices – you have to get it. I don't make the rules.

There are companies that make gin advent calendars, where you get a different gin to taste each day (a tiny bottle of each) in the weeks leading up to Christmas. A nice early present to buy for yourself or to share with someone in your household. What a way to count down!

For some reason, a gin-gin mule captures the festive spirit for me. I think it's because when I was a kid, Christmas was the time we always drank the fancy ginger beer in a glass bottle. If you don't have that same association, perhaps you can think of an equally nostalgic Christmas celebratory feeling . . . and tweak it to include gin.

Late on Christmas Eve or Christmas night, when the world has gone quiet and the decorations are twinkling in the semi-darkness, a piece of Christmas cake goes well with the cozy warmth of barrel-aged gin drank neat. Just sayin'.

Watching films

The Thin Man (1934) – Mix a dry martini or two. Serve in a Nick & Nora glass, if at all possible. I don't recommend you follow the couple's example by having six in a row.

Casablanca (1942) – Get some champagne and lemon juice and make a French 75. You don't mind drinking the Nazi's drink, do you? If it makes you feel better, you can channel Bogart – throw on a white tux, thump the desk, and lament: 'Of all the gin joints in all the towns in all the world . . . she walks into mine.'

North by Northwest (1959) – I'm not sure Cary Grant ever gets to actually enjoy his gibson, but you don't have to suffer the same fate. Just don't get caught up twirling the glass, lifting it to your lips, getting interrupted by a flirtatious companion before you can take a sip, cleaning your sunglasses, getting distracted several more times . . .

Meet the Parents (1992) – If it isn't too cringey for you, watch this comedy with a Tom Collins in hand; it's the preferred drink of De Niro's character. Or, if you can't handle hearing Ben Stiller riff about milking a cat, watch Casino instead, where De Niro uses Tom Collins as an alias to stash two million dollars in a safety deposit box.

The Great Gatsby (2013) – Mix up a tray of gin rickeys, and tell your friends this drink is mentioned by name in the book. Say it several times to make sure they hear you. Perhaps have a copy of the book on you and direct them to chapter seven, just in case they don't believe you. They'll praise your knowledge of literature. They probably won't get annoyed and leave.

Listening to vinyl

The air is thick and the jazz is smooth, so you want an equally smooth drink: a straight-down-the-line dry martini, heavy on the juniper and light on the vermouth, with a bowl of peanuts on the side. Soaking in Miles Davis and martinis, chomping down on an olive each time you flip the record over. Not many ways this evening could get better.

Or if it's more upbeat instrumental jazz – in my collection, that's Wardell Gray or Dave Brubeck – go with an old fashioned. Something with orange notes to match the twist will really sing.

Reading James Bond novels

Ian Fleming wrote 14 James Bond books, and they're a rollicking good time (even if Fleming's treatment of women and other races is a little, ahem . . . outdated).

This one's a no-brainer, since Fleming invented the Vesper in *Casino Royale*. It'd be a shame not to honour his memory by sipping on one while reading about Bond going through the ringer for the umpteenth time.

Unfortunately, the Bond films don't feature a lot of gin – mostly champagne, whisky and vodka martinis (why?!). But there's a negroni in *Dr. No*, and Bond starts drinking Vespers in the Daniel Craig films, so feel free to join him for a drink there.

Writing a book

Sitting in the dark with just the glow of your laptop screen, sipping a pink gin or two fingers of navy strength gin in a tumbler with a splash of water, writing a book . . . if you're an extrovert or you hate looking at a screen, this might sound like a nightmare to you. But if you enjoy your own company and you love working on creative projects, it's dreamy.

It even works if the book you're writing is about gin.

Making gin and food work together

'What food pairs best with gin?' isn't an easy question.

What botanicals are at the forefront of the gin? Do you prefer sweet or savoury? Are you drinking the gin with soda or with tonic, as a short intense cocktail or as a long refreshing cocktail? What shape of plate are you eating from? Was the juniper picked during a full moon? Do you plan on swimming within 30 minutes of eating?

Let go of the idea of 'right' and 'wrong'. Throw rules out the window and just play around in the kitchen. What gin drink would you pair with spiced fruit buns? What gin would you use to make pickles? What gin could you use in a salad dressing?

This is your chance to bring glorious gin and magnificent food together with three other ingredients: ideas, imagination and inspiration.

Gin marmalade or jam

Who said your enjoyment of gin couldn't start at breakfast? (Done responsibly and in moderation, of course.)

Homemade jams and marmalades are always good, but you can dial their awesomeness up a notch with a healthy dose of the good stuff. Gin and ginger make for a dynamite combo. Lime and gin will make a marmalade that channels a gimlet cocktail. And who could resist a blood orange marmalade made with orange-scented gin? Especially if it's then dolloped into a Paddington's negroni sour.

Meanwhile, if you make your own sloe gin, use the leftover gin-soaked berries to make a jam worthy of 18th-century English farmers. Pineapple gin jam will have Snoop Dogg knocking on your door, sniffing around for gin and juice. Plum and fig jam made with barrel-aged gin will evoke a boozy Christmas pudding that is, as Aunty Marge always says, 'Too good for children.'

Gin and gingerbread

During gin's dark days, London street vendors would sell gin and gingerbread for people to sip and munch as they watched public executions. They must have had iron stomachs. Either that, or the streets were even more filthy than usual at the end of those days.

But we can redeem gin and gingerbread. Get some dark gingerbread – the sticky stuff that's made with brown sugar and molasses and is more cake than cookie – and gin with a splash of soda water or bitter lemon, and let the combo give you some fire in the belly when it's cold. We served gin and gingerbread at our winter house warming (pun intended) and nary a face was downturned.

Or if you're sick and in need of some cheering, try a gin and ginger hot toddy – gin, fresh squeezed lemon juice, hot water, sugar syrup, spices and fresh ginger. Gingerbread optional.

Martini risotto

Vermouth risotto is a thing – replace the white wine in any recipe with dry vermouth, and it gives an aromatic kick to the dish.

Or you can use gin – choose a dry gin with herbaceous botanicals (e.g. rosemary, basil, lemon myrtle, coriander), use half the amount as you would wine and make up the other half with extra stock. Add finely chopped fresh rosemary when you're softening the onions and garlic, and grate lemon zest through near the end. When it's done, take it off the heat and toss through an extra shot of gin so it really pops. Garnish the risotto with a lemon twist if you're feeling cute.

But if you're ready to be clever and classy and have an amazing night, make martini risotto. A litre (34 fl oz) of stock, 400 g (14 oz) risotto rice, 150 ml (5 fl oz) gin and 150 ml (5 fl oz) dry white vermouth. Soften onions and garlic in olive oil, add the rice and stir through the gin and vermouth, gradually add stock until it's all absorbed and rice is tender (use extra water if needed). Add a few handfuls of baby spinach leaves for colour and texture – stirred, not shaken.

Non-negotiable: drink a martini while making this. Garnish both drink and dish with green Sicilian olives.

Gin and pasta

You've heard of penne alla vodka? This is penne alla gin. Traditionally, this sauce is made with cream and tomato; the vodka helps the sauce come together, keeping the tomato and cream from separating. But why use flavourless vodka when gin can enhance the flavour of the tomato? Look for dry gins with notes like savoury, peppery, herbaceous, tomato or lemon.

Pasta al limone is another traditional Italian dish that's prime for gin. Most recipes are creamy (where the gin will help as above), but my preference is lemon and olive oil – the oil lets the lemon be the star in a way that cream (or butter or cheese) don't. Find the best lemons you can (home-grown are ideal) and choose a citrus-forward gin. Toss the gin through at the end to let the brightness come through . . . as long as you don't mind your pasta dish having potent booze content.

Gin sorbet

Plenty of options here.

- **Gin and tonic sorbet** – gin, tonic and sugar, and your choice of lemon, lime or cucumber.

- **Gin sorbet with fruit infused simple syrup** – anything from berries to citrus or something more exotic like kaffir lime, dragon fruit, ginger or pineapple.

- **Sloe gin sorbet** – sloe gin and blackberries or plums. Even better if you soak the fruit in gin first . . .

- **Or simply pour a shot glass of gin over a scoop of lemon sorbet** for a simple and indulgent summer dessert. Better than an after-dinner mint.

Gin cake

For my birthday one year, a friend made me a vanilla cake with gin in the icing and layers of jam and gin-infused berries. Can recommend.

Alternatively, make a rich, orange-infused almond meal cake spiked with sweet red vermouth. Cover it with slices of blood orange drizzled with gin and made sticky with sugar. Serve with a dollop of thick natural/Greek yoghurt swirled with Campari syrup. Figured it out yet? You've got yourself a negroni cake.

Or transform a lemon drizzle cake into a gin and tonic cake: make the batter effervescent with tonic water for a fluffy, air-filled lemon sponge; drizzle it with a confusingly boozy concoction of gin, tonic and powdered sugar; cover the lot with lemon icing, spiked with a tablespoon of sweet, citrus-forward gin.

Birthdays will never be the same again.

Gin jelly

You thought champagne jelly was decadent . . . how about French 75 jelly? You don't need to make the gin-champagne cocktail to the full proportions, but add gin and lemon juice to a champagne jelly recipe. Serve in coupe glasses, each with a lemon twist balanced on the edge.

Or make a G&T jelly and line the mould with lime wheels and thin cucumber rings before pouring the jelly. For a nice textural detail, put the tonic (or champagne) in the freezer for half an hour before you start – this helps keep the bubbles in the jelly.

Honestly, you could take any gin cocktail and jellify it with the addition of a gelling agent. I dare you to. Better done for a fancy dinner party than as jelly shots, in my opinion.

Trifle

- Gin in the jam?
- Gin in the cake?
- Gin in the jelly?
- Gin in the custard?
- Gin-soaked fruit?
- Gin drizzled over the top at the end?

Take your pick. Don't do all of them, or someone will propose a new Gin Act.

A matched meal

Plan a multi-course meal paired with various gin-based drinks. Choose botanicals that suit the cuisines, and be thoughtful in how you match dishes to drinks – some dishes could use contrasting flavours, while others use complementary flavours. (To use my incredible fashion knowledge as an example, this is the difference between mixing patterns and wearing denim on denim.)

Indian – look for a gin heavy with spices like cardamom, cinnamon, nutmeg and saffron, and use it to spike a mango lassi or a post-dinner chai tea. To accompany your main dishes, a gin rickey could replace the lime pickle, or a G&T garnished with cucumber could have a cooling effect if your curry is packing heat.

Greek – lemon potatoes with a Tom Collins, and a mint-forward gin and tonic with moussaka. Finish off with an aniseed-focused gin on the rocks instead of ouzo.

Mexican – garnish a gin sour with a chilli sliced lengthways and a dusting of smoked paprika, and it'll pair beautifully with rich molé sauce. Or start from the other direction, and mess with a couple of familiar Mexican drinks – make a margarita with a coriander-heavy gin instead of tequila or dose a jug of sangria with sloe gin. Then stuff yourself on tortilla chips and guacamole and load up your tacos with fragrant herbs and plenty of salsa fresca. And if some of those herbs end up in your drink, so be it.

section four

Want more practical advice about gin, how to drink it and how to keep developing your love of the stuff?

Here's my FAQ (Fake Asked Questions).

Ask Mick

Q **I'm still new to gin, and I kind of think it all tastes the same. Where do I start?**

First of all: there's no pressure to drink gin a certain way. If at any point you find one gin brand you like and want to stick with it, or you decide you're happy ordering a gin and tonic with whatever gin's available . . . congratulations! You're enjoying gin! That's the goal!

But if you want to go further . . .

To get a handle on classic gin, the big historical gins are a solid place to start. Gordon's, Tanqueray and Beefeater are well-established brands with great quality control and consistency, and have been around for hundreds of years, so they've set the standard for 'that traditional gin flavour'.

Once you've tried these, check out gins from your region. Go to a cool small bar and ask them to recommend a local gin and tell you about it. Even better if there's a local craft distillery and you can talk to somebody who makes the gin. Failing that, the internet makes it easy to find and buy gins made in your country, or city, or neighbourhood.

As for how to try these gins, I'd go about it the following way:

Taste it on its own. That may seem a little confronting at first, but you can do it. Be slow and thoughtful in the way you taste it (see 'Tasting gin' on page 117). You can either try this on your own, or with friends who want to get into gin.

After that, see how the character of gin comes through in a variety of mixed drinks and cocktails. I recommend the following drinks, all made on a dry gin:

- **A long gin and tonic,** made with a ratio of 1:4 (perhaps 50 ml [1⅔ fl oz] gin to 200 ml [6⅔ fl oz] tonic). This is the most popular way people drink gin.

- **A short gin and tonic,** made with a ratio of 1:1. By changing the ratio, you'll understand what part the gin is playing, and what part the tonic water is playing.

- **A Tom Collins** – tall and refreshing.

- **A dry martini** – short and strong.

- **A negroni** – bitter and sweet.

- **A gin sour** – sour, but also smooth when done well.

Either make these drinks at home or go to a decent gin or cocktail bar where you trust they'll make the classics well. It may help to tell the bartender you specifically want classic versions of these drinks, so they don't serve you their signature version made with cask-aged pineapple gin and garnished with roasted plums.

After you've done all this, you can revisit these drinks with different brands and alterations, or you can explore different cocktails, or different styles of gin, different distilleries, different mixers, different mixing ratios, different garnishes . . . there truly are infinite opportunities for experimentation.

Q Can I make my own gin?

Distilling alcohol is tightly regulated in pretty much every country. One reason is because governments do not like unregulated explosions and poison, which can result when distilling isn't done the right way. Another reason is because governments do like taxes, so they don't want people making alcohol that isn't being taxed. In most countries, distilling isn't legal unless you have the appropriate licence.

But distilling isn't your only option.

You can infuse vodka with botanicals or botanical essences at home to make gin. Or you can make sloe gin or gin liqueur by bringing together gin with sugar and sloe berries or other flavouring ingredients. You just need a big jar and some patience. And a recipe – the internet is your friend here.

Some distilleries run classes and workshops where you can make your own gin, whether it's taking part in the distilling process or just mixing botanical extracts with neutral spirit.

Others will allow you to order a tailor-made gin online, where you choose which botanicals are in the gin and at what strengths – all from the comfort of your couch.

Q I don't like tonic water.

That's not a question. But okay. We can work with that.

It's probably the bitterness that you don't like. (You may also dislike negronis, which feature Campari made with Italian bitter oranges.)

Bitterness is an acquired taste. No-one likes bitter things when they're a kid, but many adults develop a love of black coffee, dark chocolate, beer and red wine. And gin and tonic.

So if you'd like to acquire a taste for tonic water, you can. Try making G&Ts with less tonic water at first – you can cut your drink with soda water, or just drink a stronger ratio of gin to tonic.

You've got to want it – by definition, it will involve drinking something that you don't yet enjoy, so you need to have the right mindset to do it. And you've got to stick with it – the more G&Ts you have, the more different tonic waters you taste, the more other bitter foods and drinks you try, the more your tastes will change. I mean this literally; your tastebuds physically change shape with time and exposure to different tastes.

On the other hand, there's no rule saying you *should* acquire a taste for tonic water. You could go the rest of your life drinking gin with soda water or other mixers, or as cocktails, and never touch a drop of tonic water. And while I can't guarantee anything, I *think* you'd be fine.

Ⓠ How do I run a gin event or gin club?

The gin club I was part of consisted of a small group of friends – about six of us were regulars.

We'd meet up one evening a month.

We'd have three or four gins. Sometimes they followed a theme (all from the same distillery, or the same country, or all featuring a particular botanical), but just as often they were unrelated but interesting looking gins.

With each, we'd smell it and taste it neat. Without any outside input, we'd talk about what we could smell, what we could taste.

Once we'd done that, we'd look at a flavour wheel, and see if that helped us to articulate what we were smelling and tasting. We'd also look at the tasting notes for that gin from the label, the distillery's website, and sometimes even online reviews.

We'd then each add a splash of something to our gin – either room temperature water, or cold water, or soda water, or tonic water – or an ice cube. We'd talk through the flavours again, and how they'd been affected (or not) by what we added.

Once we'd worked our way through each of the gins, we'd all have a pre-selected cocktail using the gin we decided would go best in it.

But there's no one way to run something like this. Here are some more ideas:

You could start with a tasting pack from a distillery or other online service.

Find an online distillery tour, or video of a master distiller running through a tasting.

Taste one gin with several tonics and garnishes. Or different mixers. Or as different cocktails.

Try running a blind tasting game. One person brings a few gins, but keeps them secret. They print or write out tasting notes or online reviews of the gins, but without any hints of which gin is which. Then they serve the gins to the other people, who have no idea what the gins are. Everyone tastes the gin neat or with a splash of water/soda, and tries to match up each secret gin with its respective tasting notes.

Botanicals tasting! Get your hands on as many botanicals as you reasonably can – maybe a range of citrus fruits or a range of fresh spices (e.g. nutmeg you crush yourself) from a bulk food store or Indian spice shop. Smell or taste each botanical as appropriate. Discuss them, describe them and try to familiarise yourself with them. Take turns closing your eyes and having someone else wave a botanical under your nose and trying to distinguish what you're smelling.

Is there non-alcoholic gin?

Sure is!

Well, technically, it's not classified as 'gin'. But there are distilled non-alcoholic spirits where the maker has either distilled gin and then de-alcoholised it, or distilled juniper and other botanicals with water. But we can call it non-alc gin here. Don't tell the fuzz.

At the time of writing, Gordon's and Tanqueray both make non-alcoholic gins. There are also other brands that have launched specifically as non-alcoholic brands that make a gin-like spirit, such as Atopia, with botanical non-alc spirits (created by Hendrick's master distiller Leslie Grace) that are 'best served with tonic.'

Ask around at your local bottle shop. Or online, of course – there are whole online stores dedicated to non-alc alternatives that will have a range of 'gins' and recommendations, as well as non-alc ingredients like 'vermouth' and 'bitter red aperitif' that you can use in non-alcoholic gin cocktails.

Does non-alcoholic gin taste the same as the hard stuff? The short answer is 'No' – the alcohol in a gin drink affects the flavour, not just your desire to have a nap. (Although, fun fact: some brands of non-alc gin use a small amount of capsaicin or chilli to simulate the alcoholic burn.)

But if you'd like to drink a gin-like beverage with tonic or a non-alc cocktail, you can. Don't expect it to be cheap, and don't expect the same complexity and intensity as an alcoholic gin. Simply enjoy it for what it is.

Q Can I see how gin is made?

Your best bet is to look into the distilleries closest to you. They may run tours or gin-making experiences, or you can just talk with the owner or distiller and ask questions. If you ask nicely, they might even give you a peek behind the scenes. That's the beauty of small distilleries – they give you the chance to connect with the maker and tap into their gin knowledge.

You can also find plenty of videos online – interviews with master distillers, walkthroughs of the gin-making process and virtual tours of distilleries.

Q What does juniper taste like?

These little berries are complex beasts, and the answer to this question is similarly complex.

Some descriptors for juniper include: piney, woody, spicy, citrus, floral, peppery, camphor, antiseptic, menthol, turpentine, waxy, resinous, herbal, bitter, sweet, savoury, oily, balsamic, musty, minty, nutmeg, rosemary, heather, earthy, lavender, banana.

There are variables like the species of juniper, where the juniper was grown and the moisture content of the berries; these all affect what essential oils are in the juniper, and shape how intensely each flavour shows through.

And when the flavour molecules from the juniper interact with alcohol and flavour compounds from other botanicals, they can taste different again.

Did that clear it up for you?

If gin is the only way you've experienced juniper, it may not be easy to pinpoint the juniper flavours in gin anyway. After all, the beauty of a well-made gin is that the flavours blend so well together, and gin makers often intentionally choose botanicals that have overlapping flavours with gin. It's part of the art of making a balanced gin.

But keep tasting juniper-forward gins and articulating the flavours you're picking up, and in time you should start to get a sense of when that piney-antiseptic, woody-floral, spicy-peppery, citrussy-resinous flavour is coming from the juniper.

Simple, right?

Q I struggle to pick out tasting notes in gin. What's wrong with me?

Nothing, probably. I mean, it's possible you have some rare tastebud disease – I don't know your medical history. But more likely you have healthy tastebuds, but you haven't yet developed a palate for gin.

A well-made gin is often designed to weave flavours together seamlessly, so it can be hard to distinguish them from each other. Or to switch metaphors: the aromatics and flavours blend together like the sounds of different instruments in an orchestra. Some people are better at recognising the sounds of the string section from the brass section, or following the bass line and the melody, or commenting on which particular woodwind instrument is their favourite.

You can improve your tasting skills with practice. Try side-by-side tastings of a few gins with markedly different styles so you're more likely to be able to taste the difference: say, a London dry, a barrel-aged, and something contemporary with wacky botanicals in it. Once you've mastered that, try side-by-side tastings of a few contemporary gins with different botanical profiles. As your palate develops, you could move towards tasting similar gins (e.g. three London dry gins) and see if you can pick up the nuances of flavours.

Just take your time and pay attention, and you'll train your palate. Chase down a gin flavour wheel if you want some guidance in finding the right words. But if you never get past describing a gin as 'piney' or 'citrussy', who cares? To return to the orchestra metaphor: you don't have to pick out the notes that the second violin is playing in order to enjoy the symphony.

Does gin go bad?

The short answer is: no, gin won't go 'off'. But it will slowly deteriorate in flavour once it's been opened.

The longer answer is: unopened gin more or less has an unlimited shelf life. Heat and light can affect it, but as long as it's not stored somewhere hot (like next to the oven) or in direct sunlight, it should remain largely unaffected even if stored for years and years. But unlike some wines, it doesn't improve with age, so there's no point cellaring it.

Once a bottle of gin has been opened, it will start to deteriorate. It's not a quick process. But oxygen slowly breaks down some of the flavour molecules from the botanicals, and every time you open the bottle some of those aroma compounds succeed in escaping.

If you store your gin correctly (cool, dark place; consistent temperature; lid screwed on tightly) it'll be close to its best for a year. I'd recommend enjoying it before the second year has passed.

But the botanicals in gin will be brightest when the bottle is freshly opened and will subtly change as time ticks on. A few months or a year isn't a problem, but don't bother with that half-full bottle of Gordon's you inherited from your grandma in 1993.

If you're not working through a bottle of gin very quickly, I recommend inviting friends over to share it with you. Everyone loves a gin party, and all gin tastes better shared with friends anyway.

So what are you waiting for? Enjoy your gin now – there's no time like the present!

Ⓠ Where do I go from here?

Get to know other gin drinkers. Go to your local gin bar and make friends with other punters and with the staff. Go to events and masterclasses and gin festivals. Join online communities and chat on forums. Send a message to your favourite gin bloggers and Instagrammers (Ginstagrammers?).

Where possible, talk to the people who make and sell gin. Visit distilleries whenever you get the chance, and see the passion in the eyes of people who see gin as more than just a product. Ask questions about their gin, and the botanicals they use, and their production process and how best to drink their gin. Enthusiasm is just as important as knowledge.

Having said that: chase down more knowledge. The internet is an excellent resource: check out the Gin Guild and *Gin Magazine* to keep up to date with the world of gin; check out The GIN is IN website for hundreds of detailed gin reviews; check out Difford's Guide for excellent information and cocktail recipes. Read articles galore. And, of course, read books about gin, spirits in general and cocktails. Build your own personal gin library.

Find gin experiences. Go to tastings, distillery tours and gin-making workshops. Check out the gin scene when you travel overseas. You could even plan an international (ginternational?) gin tour with friends!

Make your own gin experiences. Organise a distillery crawl. Host a gin tasting. Start a gin club. Find yourself a flavour wheel or chart that you find useful, and work at distinguishing various botanical flavours. Keep a gin journal and reflect on the gins you drink with notes about the botanicals, aromas and flavours.

Taste a lot of gins. Try a lot of cocktails. Geek out about gin with anyone who's interested.

And the most important thing? Keep having fun with gin. You don't always need to be dissecting the gin you're drinking. Sometimes you can make a G&T without measuring the ratio – le gasp! – and unwind without thinking about the flavour notes. Or break the rules when you make a martini. It's cool to take gin seriously at times, but you can take a break from that, too. Sir Alfred Juniper of Lesterfordshire* didn't invent gin to only ever be treated like a carefully monitored science experiment. He invented it to be enjoyed. Honour his memory by stopping sometimes to just enjoy a blissful glass of gin – however you want to.

*This may not be a real historical figure.

Acknowledgements

So much gratitude, so little space . . .

The Rockpool Publishing crew – especially Lisa and Paul, for their confidence and investment in me, and Luke, for chasing me up just enough (but not too much).

The designers who make my work look good, the editors who make my words flawless, the sales and distribution teams . . . these people are the reason you're holding a beautiful book instead of reading a word document on a screen.

Ellie Grant, for the inspired (and super fun!) illustrations that make my words much more colourful.

Justin Reddy, who let me shadow him for hours while he made gin and patiently answered all my questions . . . and then later read what I wrote to make sure I didn't say anything stupid.

Jimmy Young, who let me rock up to Milton Common and use it as my personal photo studio.

Muzza and Knives at The Twin. Thanks for the coffee, the chats and for letting me wear a butt-shaped groove in your seats.

My wife Kamina. She dedicated hours of her time to help me research, lent her creativity and wit when I needed inspiration, experimented with gimlets late at night, and put up with my absence (physically and mentally) when I was racing to finish this book . . . and she did all of this with a new baby. What an absolute champion.

I suppose my baby boy should get a mention here, too. He actually made writing this book harder, not easier . . . but I'm so glad he showed up. He makes me smile, constantly.

About the author

Mick Wüst is an award-winning drinks writer who's been writing about booze since 2015. When he's not drinking beer or gin for work, he's eating bread and drinking coffee for fun.

Mick's worked as a pastor, a lecturer and a barista, and he runs semi-often to keep the beer belly at bay. He lives in Brisbane (the best city) with his wife and son (the best people).

His first book, *Beer Drinker's Toolkit*, is just as good as this one. Possibly better, as it contains a naughty joke.